I'd Do It Again!

I'd Do It Again!

-A Memoir-

Harriet Wright with Brie Austin

iUniverse, Inc.
New York Lincoln Shanghai

I'd Do It Again!
-A Memoir-

iUniverse books may be ordered through booksellers or by contacting:

iUniverse
2021 Pine Lake Road, Suite 100
Lincoln, NE 68512
www.iuniverse.com
1-800-Authors (1-800-288-4677)

ISBN-13: 978-0-595-36492-3 (pbk)
ISBN-13: 978-0-595-80925-7 (ebk)
ISBN-10: 0-595-36492-6 (pbk)
ISBN-10: 0-595-80925-1 (ebk)

Printed in the United States of America

DEDICATED TO;

Don; the love of my life,

George; the most important man in my life, and

Clovis; my son, my heart

Acknowledgments

A SPECIAL THANK YOU to those that helped make this book a reality:

Sarah Montague, Roxanne Lowit, Rosie Loew, Nikki Haskell, Charlotte Dennett and Jerry Colby, Lynn Montano, Rimsky Dartigue, Jim Berry, Diana DeFelippi, and of course my co-writer; Brie Austin

Contents

PROLOGUE

Murray and Me...
Life on the Glamorous Track

The phone rang early on a May morning. When I picked it up, and said hello, I got the shock of my life: It was Margie calling to tell me that Murray, the Mafia bookie, the nightclub denizen, Murray my constant companion, roommate and meal ticket for eight years—my Murray, whom I threw out over 30 years earlier, was dead.

It was now 1985, and Murray had been in Chicago since the 1950s, for nearly all the years since I left him, or rather politely asked him to leave the New York apartment we shared. There was a time in those crazy years after World War II, when I lost a husband, raised a baby boy, and kept up with the nightclub set, when Murray became a vital part of my everyday life. We were a couple: regulars at the Copacabana, Latin Quarter, 21, and all the fashionable night spots where Murray conducted his business and I chatted with celebrities.

I was Murray's companion, and he was my live-in benefactor. For eight years it was a mutually agreeable arrangement. But, then Murray had decamped to Chicago because of a dispute with some Mafia friends over money he owed them. Except for a brief visit I made a few years later, I hadn't heard from him since.

Now I felt I owed him something. In times past when I needed help and a friend, Murray was there, even though he never required a thank you. I knew there would be no family there, he never maintained a relationship with them. So it still seemed my place. I caught the next flight to Chicago.

Immediately I went to get Murray's keys from Margie and Howie Wong, his best friends. Next, I headed right for Murray's apartment on Lake Shore Drive, one of the better sections of Chicago. Most people would have been stunned

1

by Murray's home. Not I. I always associated Murray with gorgeous apartments that had white rugs, ornate furniture, expensive curtains, lamps and original artwork. He was always redecorating our New York apartment, often on the spur of the moment. He had expensive—if flashy—taste and was no cheapskate: he bought only the best.

His Chicago apartment proved he hadn't changed. Everything was white, not only the rugs, but all the furniture as well. The couch had white satin pillows, the tables were glass, and the custom-made draperies were closed to keep out the light and block the view of Lake Michigan. Murray, like me, had seen the best of the glitz era, and he wanted to keep it that way.

In the kitchen, I couldn't resist checking the refrigerator. What I saw was typical: lots of chocolate candy and ice cream. Murray only snacked at home; he dined out for every meal. A side-room, perhaps a pantry, was filled with all sorts of electrical cooking gadgets from Hammacher Schlemmer (a specialty store for the rich)—this from a man who couldn't hammer a nail.

I was helping Margie take inventory, when the phone rang. I answered, and a surly, raspy voice asked, "What are you doing in that apartment? I wanna talk to you…" It doesn't take much to get my Irish temper up. "Listen," I said, "if you have anything to say to me, come talk to me eyeball to eyeball." I hung up. I wasn't afraid of anybody out there. But, I knew I'd have company soon. Margie left to return to work, so I was alone when this little Al Capone type— squinty eyes, no neck, large cigar, big hat, and a limp—came strolling down the hallway. The apartment door was open, so he came in, peering around to see if he knew me, and if anyone else was there. I waited. When he got ready to say something, I got there first.

"Look, before you say anything, sit down." He sat. "I'm no whore Murray hooked up with," I said, "we go back 40 years. I'm here to see that Murray gets a good funeral. That's what I came out here to do. OK?" I was speaking calmly. He remained silent. "I don't know who you are or what you want here," I continued. "Are you here to help?" The little guy thought a moment…then nodded yes. "First thing we do, we check him out of the hospital," he said, in a casual way as if we were going to rent a car. "Then we'll get him over to this funeral parlor that some friends of mine have, so we can set up the wake properly."

The funeral parlor was owned by the Italian mob—however, I wasn't about to argue that issue right now. We went to the hospital, signed some papers, and arranged to have Murray brought to the funeral home. It never occurred to me that Murray being Jewish could be a problem after he died. It had never been a problem when he was alive. All the mob guys called him "Little Moishe", but that was about it.

Little Al," whose name turned out to be Rocco got the ball rolling: The wake was to take two days and nights, with the funeral to follow on the third morning in the Our Lady of Something-or-other cemetery. Fine! I knew none of these people, although it was obvious that his old mob friends still had special affection for Murray. Most people who knew him did. He had never been a typical "dese" and "doze" mob guy. He had been a quiet, gentlemanly guy with a strong sense of duty. So now I considered my duty to be that of seeing Murray properly buried, then I could go home.

But first, there was the wake on Thursday and Friday. It was suggested by Rocco that it would be a "good thing" if I could be in the front row of mourners to greet the visitors, as Murray had no family. OK by me…anything to move things along. The wake was a picture of floral excess—Murray would have loved it. Roses ($600 worth) adorned the head of the casket with another $600 arrangement placed at the foot. Other bouquets, wreaths and clusters sat in baskets and huge vases atop tables, which occupied every niche and corner of the room. The ornately carved casket had a white shirred lining and seemed to rest on a huge wave of flowers. The room was decorated in an ornate style—heavy red drapes, red furniture a large-patterned carpeting. Soft Italian music was played throughout the room and into the side rooms. Murray himself seemed lost in these surroundings. He looked smaller than I remembered, and his white hair disappeared in the colorlessness white appearance of his flesh.

During the wake itself, with a steady stream of people coming and going, you could hear the constant buzz of voices, too low to distinguish what was being said. But there was the atmosphere that is always present at a wake attended by people about the same age as the guest of honor in the coffin. You get the feeling of, "Who's next?" Mourners, almost exclusively men well dressed who stood around in small groups whispering to one another, took up spaces not occupied by all the over-furnishing. Occasionally, someone from one knot of mourners would ease over to another group and wedge himself into the conversation.

All who spoke to me did so with deference. In effect, I was the token woman. Many of them I knew immediately, Guys I recognized from California, Vegas, New York, all came to pay their respects. At least I remembered their faces, because I never knew the real names of Murray's associates. But, all those Italian faces and star sapphire pinky rings were vivid reminders of my life with Murray. So were the money filled envelopes passed quietly to Murray's pizan, Rocco, on the receiving line. Rocco was the treasurer. I received none of these tokens of respect, but I didn't expect or want any of it. I just wanted to get this over with so I could go home, but my post-Murray adventure wasn't over yet.

After the first evening of the wake, I was back at the apartment ready for bed, when the phone rang. "Now, what do they want?" I asked myself as I picked up the phone. "You don't know us," a strange voice said calmly. "We're friends of Murray."

"Yes?"

"Yes. But we're his Jewish friends, from Las Vegas. Murray was Jewish," he said. I realized where this conversation was heading. "I know, but I couldn't tell the mob guys what to do." He interrupted, "We know all about that, so don't worry. But, we want to get Murray out of that funeral home and into a Jewish one so we can sit Shiva." This was shaping up as something I wanted to be far away from, and I said so. "Look, you guys fight this out among yourselves. Leave me out of it. By the end of the week, I'm getting on a plane for New York. I just want to see Murray buried. You guys can settle where and by whom."

I skipped the Italian wake that night because I was asked to sit with the Jewish mourners. This was the Las Vegas mob that arrived en masse soon after my conversation with Little Al's counterpart, Kenny. After talking to me, they went to the Italian funeral home, long after visiting hours—and took away Murray's corpse. It was a comedy of errors

I wasn't surprised that the Vegas mob took over. I wouldn't have been surprised if we suddenly heard from the New York mob, and I had another wake to go to. Murray would have been touched by all the attention of grief and respect he was getting from the organization.

The Jewish funeral was a stark contrast to the previous evening's opulent wake. The funeral parlor was very plain, if not bare. Wooden chairs arranged in rows, facing a simple wooden unlined casket. Murray now wore a yarmulke and what looked like a simple robe. I couldn't help wondering if this simply furnished funeral parlor had ever before hosted a deceased who was first embalmed and had been the featured guest at an Italian wake. This was hardly in keeping with Jewish tradition, so it's probably just as well that they didn't know.

It seemed as if the Las Vegas group won out in whatever negotiations they had over Murray's body, because the next morning, a limo picked me up and took me to the gravesite they had picked in a Jewish cemetery. I didn't recognize anyone. The crowd was large and didn't mingle much. I felt very lonely and sad, and more than ready to leave. But before going home I had to pack up Murray's things and make arrangements to get rid of the apartment. The Chicago boys told me to take whatever I wanted of Murray's effects.

Like Murray's décor, his closet was a shrine to old-fashioned excess: I packed 250 shirts, 100 suits, 60 pairs of shoes (some still in boxes), coats, jackets, lots of Cavanaugh hats (these fedora-like hats were a sign of high style in

Murray's circle), and jewelry—gold watches, cufflinks (gold and platinum) and everything else a man about town would wear. It took boxes and boxes to pack it all, though some of the clothes wound up adorning his Chicago chums. All these belongings, and the furniture, went to Marge and Howie's apartment—except for a small box I packed for myself—including a gold Cartier watch given to him by Hugh Heffner, which I still wear today.

Much of this is what you might expect from anyone's house, but I thought I'd find one or two signs of Murray's unorthodox lifestyle. Whenever he was short of cash, an occupational hazard in his business, he'd pawn something valuable, and reclaim it when he was flush again, so pawn tickets, or hock tickets, as he called them, were always to be found among Murray's personal things. Out of curiosity, I searched for some, but none were to be found.

When I finally finished the apartment was totally empty, another door, another life closed. I caught the next plane back to New York. My conscience was clear. I had done what I wanted, to honor Murray for the past, and now I could get on with my life. I had no idea what was in store for me, and that's a good thing. My life was due for a dramatic about face, about as far from the Murray's, the mob, and the Copacabana as you can get. But, I'm getting ahead of myself…

CHAPTER 1

A Time Of Excess

At the age of eighty-eight, I don't have the time nor the patience for bullshit. Not that I ever did. As a child I remember my mother saying, "don't tell me, show me," and in many ways I guess that concept stuck with me. "What's done is done, gone is gone," she'd say. It is a phrase I find myself reciting to others quite often.

I met with adversity early in life. In the first weeks I almost died. I also suffered broken bones and the loss of sight in one eye from the measles—all before I was three years old. But then everyone has some adversity in his or her life; I was no exception. To some degree I have always believed that while some people are born lucky, others determine the course of their own lives by the decisions they make. I was somewhere in the middle. I never had a definitive plan; my life was sort of a journey in free form. I lived in the moment, but not necessarily for it, and as a result, every time one door closed another suddenly appeared before me.

I've known many people in my life that have lived long enough to have had regrets and they tell me, "I should have done this or I could have done that." I don't want to be redundant but what's done is done, "Get over it and move on," I tell them. Some people however, are resigned to sit in heaven's waiting room while the world passes them by. They exchange the rest of their life to relive distorted memories of better times, failing to realize that they are in fact still alive. Isn't it funny how memories have a way of sometimes making things— and people—better than they were? I have some great memories, but I don't live for them. I enjoy them, but I live in the now, in this moment. When I die, I'll do it living!

I have never questioned the choices I made, but rather, embraced the road I was on and made the best of where it took me. Some choices were better than others, and yet all of it, good and bad, weaved together, became my life. My friends tell me that it was different than most—so many adventures, such highs and such lows. They would, and do, wonder how I did it all in one lifetime. "Because I live, I don't sit," I say. People have insisted that I should write a book, so finally, I did. This is my life.

I was born in the early 20th century on April 15, 1917, in Brooklyn New York—just nine days before the United States plunged into World War I, the Great War as they called it. It was a turbulent time, which should have given my mother some indication of what she was in for with me. With her hectic schedule she must have lost track of when I was due, but certainly realized it when she felt severe stomach pains. Next thing she knew delivery had begun. Wobbling to a chair in the kitchen, while she held my head, she reached for the broom. She banged it on the floor to alert her husband who was working in the candy store they owned and operated directly below the apartment.

Ben came tearing upstairs and took in the scene; he saw enough to believe he had achieved fatherhood, and that his offspring was a boy! (Perhaps, he confused the unbiblical cord with something else). He rushed outside to pronounce to the world that he had a son to be named Harry, while my mother was left to call the doctor on her own. When Ben returned, the cold truth was evident: he was resigned to having a daughter named Harriet.

From the moment I was born I was a whirling dervish, always in the eye of the storm. Whether I created that storm, or was merely sought out by it, still remains unclear. But an invisible force would follow me throughout my life and provide me with an exciting—if not always fun—ride. Needy, my older sister, inquired as to "what" I was, and my mother explained that I was a special baby doll.

In those first weeks of my life I was becoming noticeably thinner, and no one could figure out why. My parents grew frantic. When they concluded that I was close to death's door they arranged for an undertaker to visit. With all the grief and tears no one thought to watch me closely over a long period of time except Grandma Weber, on hand for the deathwatch. She sat by quietly as mother prepared the usual bottle, and placed it next to my head where I could reach. Moments later—as soon as my mother left the room—she saw Needy nonchalantly pick up the bottle and chug-a-lug the milk. She returned the empty bottle back into the crib, as she had apparently done before. The mystery was solved, and within days I began to regain my health. Mother had a long talk with Needy, who couldn't comprehend what she had done wrong. "This doll is different from the other dolls you have," my mother explained to her. Needy had heard the word "doll," and took it literally. As innocent as her actions were they almost had deadly results.

After such a rocky start one could only hope that it would be smooth sailing from here. But, Needy wasn't through with me yet. By my 1st birthday I was always clamoring for attention, and on one day in particular I upstaged her, which was a big mistake. She pushed me from my high chair and I broke my left leg. For months I was the only one-year-old on my block—if not in the entire city—with a leg in a cast. And, just to keep the drama going, I had to wear a stretcher/brace because my left leg was discovered to be shorter than my right. My mother messaged Glycerin Rose Water and oil into it each night. But, to this day my left leg is still ½ inch shorter. Adversity can truly be a pain in the…leg. But what doesn't kill you makes you stronger they say, and I was undeterred.

Like most kids in the early 1900s, I was the product of immigrants. Then again, everyone was—unless of course you were a Native American Indian. People came from all over the world searching for a better life. My parents grew up on the East Coast just shortly after the "wild West" was settled. My mother, Elve, grew up in a middle class neighborhood in Brooklyn, one of six children of French, Danish and Irish decent. Though she was a petite woman in size, her confidence and extraverted personality made her large in presence. Self-taught in French and Latin—at a time when higher education was hard to come by—she was talented as well, with a beautiful singing voice and the ability to play the piano by ear. I enjoyed listening whenever I had the opportunity. Sewing and fashion design came natural to her as well, something that would have an impact on me later in life—in ways I couldn't begin to imagine.

My mother's father, Louis Weber, was always a mystery. I remember my granddad as well educated and fine: a tall elegant man who struck a strong resemblance to President Taft. He was reserved—except each July 4th when he would bring home hundreds of dollars worth of fireworks to delight the whole neighborhood with a show. He never spoke of his family, but each Sunday bought a New Orleans newspaper and read it thoroughly, paying close attention to the society columns. My mother, her sisters and brothers all had traditional southern names, and my granddad always claimed that his daughters (my mother and her sisters) were all named after his sisters. This just supported our theory that he was originally from New Orleans. I had an inquisitive—if not mischievous—mind, but I wasn't alone in my belief that granddad Weber had a dark past. In 2002, during a vacation to New Orleans to visit my cousin, I finally learned the background to who my granddad was.

In 1856 he was born Jean Luis Webre in LaFourche Parish (Thibadeaux Louisiana). The son of immigrants from Alsace-Lorraine, France on the German border, his family originally settled in St. Jean Baptiste Parish in Louisiana and proliferated in numbers. His mother's parents, wealthy landowner's, were said to have had received one of the original land grants from Louis XIV in the 1690's—the earliest record of land grants in Louisiana. Granddad was raised on his grandfathers sugar plantation, which grew from 39 to 100 slaves over ten years—the manner by which a plantations' wealth was measured. There he received private tutoring lessons from a Frenchman, who taught him seven languages. In short, he lived a charmed life.

That abruptly changed during the civil war. The slaves eventually all walked off the plantation—taking the wealth of it with them. With bi-annual taxes assessed on them, most of the plantations at that time suffered financially. By the 1880s granddad dropped out of site, and then turned up later in New York City, where he met and married my grandmother, Bridgett Johnson. She was a descendent of a Danish father and a mother born of Irish immigrants from County Sligo Ireland, who were among the tens of thousands who fled Europe during the great famine of the 1840's (as depicted in the 2002 Martin Scorsese film *"Gangs Of New York."*) Bridget also grew up in Brooklyn, but to a very poor family. She was a sweet, ordinary, woman who was very quiet, and in later years, very large—300 lbs. A regular at the local movie theater everyday, the theater manager would remove the divider from between two seats to accommodate her. If someone was sitting in "her' seat when she arrived, management would politely ask them to move.

We always wondered what brought these seemingly two different people, from different backgrounds together. So the thought prevailed—could granddad have been in hiding? Once he arrived in New York he worked for a fireworks factory, adjacent to Castle Garden, where all the immigrants at that time were processed (Ellis Island didn't open until 1896). It was an easy place for a man to mix into the crowd and disappear. The area contained some of the oldest buildings in New York City located immediately south of where the World Trade Center stood from April 4, 1973 (Ribbon cutting ceremony) until it's collapse on September 11, 2001 from a terrorist attack.

The first substantial record of Louis and Bridget (now spelled "Webber") was in the 1900 census showing them living in Brooklyn with their six children in an apartment on Baltic Street; just two short blocks from Amity Street where Winston Churchill's mother had been born some forty years earlier. They eventually settled in Cobble Hill, another area of Brooklyn. The census stated that Louis Webber was born in Ireland, a big conflict with the information that he listed on his daughter's birth certificate. Who was Jean Luis Webre~ A/K/A Louis Webber/Weber?

It turns out that in the 1880s he was involved in a dispute involving a silver mine in New Mexico. There was an exchange of gun fire that left one man dead, and it wasn't Jean Luis Webre. He stole a horse and traveled to Galveston where he hopped a steamship headed for New York City, and he never looked back. To the best of our knowledge he never contacted his family again, and it is believed that they never knew of his whereabouts.

During my childhood I knew about none of this. I spent almost every weekend at my grandparent's home and remember them fondly. I don't know how I feel with the new knowledge that grandpa Weber shot a man dead in New Mexico. Did he attack the man or did the man attack him? Was it a partner or a stranger? Whatever the truth is, all I know is that I loved him and was devastated when he passed away—I was ten years old at the time. He was at the very least a colorful character with a sorted past, who for a brief moment was part of my life.

As for Bridget, she loved to tell me stories of Irish folklore filled with mystery and intrigue. The stories were vivid and would grasp my attention as I hung on every word. Then, as I would move about the house I would do so with hesitation in fear of what was lurking behind each door. When it was time for sleep I would race down the hallway diving into my bed, never looking back. Fear can be so exhilarating and scary at the same time.

My father, Ben, was the son of Russian Jewish immigrants. When he married Elve, my mother, his parents sat shiva: a Jewish tradition after the death of a loved one. And to them Ben was dead for marrying a non-Jew. Ten years later however, they softened, due mostly to the efforts of my mother, and the power of money. When Ben had achieved a certain level of wealth she would send our chauffeur Calvin to pick them up and take them for the day to Coney Island and other sightseeing spots around the area. She went out of her way to think of them when Ben wouldn't. Slowly, my mother was looking better to them all the time—despite the fact that she wasn't a "nice Jewish girl." So we began to visit their home on Sundays for bagels, cream cheese, lox, and whitefish—my only exposure to New York Jewish culture. Ben might have been Jewish, but I wasn't. My mother was Irish Catholic, and since the Jewish culture is traced through the mother, I couldn't be considered Jewish. Still, I wasn't raised in any religious denomination at all. My mother refused to have religion in the house. She never did explain why.

I never really got to know Ben's father, there was no connection for me—something that I would come to understand later in life. He was very religious and all I remember is that he had a very long beard and always wore a yarmulke on his head. My grandmother, Bubby, stood only 4'11," the same height I would be, and I remember her fondly. She was dainty and endearing. I always wanted to take care of her, despite only being a kid myself. But she didn't need help. She was quite capable on her own. I was so impressed how clean she kept the house. It's funny the images that stick with you a lifetime later. We would always arrive at her house, and then within a short time Ben would be off to the unknown, and return to pick us up later in the day. Decades later I would learn that he spent most of that time with his many girlfriends.

Ben was extremely hard working, or more accurately, driven. In the early days, typical for the era in which I grew up, he worked during the day and then spent many nights carousing with his buddies while my mother stayed home in the apartment attending to the children. We weren't poor, but money wasn't plentiful as it would be later on. For now, the candy store was only a modest living. Ben, still in his early 20's, with four mouths to feed, was scrambling to make a name for himself. He worked hard, using the slow building profits of the store to buy other real estate, pyramiding businesses until in 1921, he bought a radio store that prospered—like other radio stores did throughout Brooklyn at that time.

This was before television, so the radio was a hot item. It was also the beginning of the "roaring 20s." What a decade—it was the Wild West and New York high society all rolled up into one: prohibition, bootleggers, rumrunners, guns, gambling, and the famous Ziegfeld Girls. Of course I was only a kid, so the only part of the 20s I got to participate in was the Charleston: the newest, hippest dance-step in all the clubs. I learned it in the streets, which is also where I learned about most things: through gossip and story telling between kids.

But that's what was great about my childhood: I had one. My mother let me be a kid, even though I continually abused that privilege. I lived at a time when kids didn't have to be adults until they were of age. We didn't always do what they wanted, but adults still enjoyed having us around, which is ironic, because as an adult I couldn't stand having kids around. In my day some kids were "street wise," but the world for us seemed much larger than for children today. We didn't have instant connectivity to global information. We couldn't watch a war being played out in front of our eyes on television (neither the television or the Internet were invented yet) nor would adults allow us to be subjected to newspaper items with adult or violent themes. In my little corner of the world I was protected by the ever-watchful eye of my mother, who kept me distanced from the atrocities of life.

When Ben started making more money from some shrewd business plans, he moved us to a new house, in a nice upper-middle class neighborhood in the Midwood section of Brooklyn. Of course I continued my antics there as well. By then Needy stopped regarding me as either a toy or a rival, and ceased picking on me. We collaborated on certain pieces of mischief in the time-honored manner of sisters, though I never had any difficulty finding ways to get into trouble on my own. There were so many things I would see or hear that I thought were ridiculous, and it would prompt me into action. I even organized a parade up East 26th Street on New Year's Eve. The band instruments were pots and pans, handed out to all the kids who wanted to join in, which I "borrowed" from a neighbor's pantry, unauthorized, you might say. The neighbor was Jewish, and she observed strict dietary laws, which meant keeping a kosher household with two sets of dishes. "Two sets of dishes! She is just trying to put on airs," I said, you know, like she was trying to hold herself out as being above other people in the neighborhood.

In my ignorance, this "I'll show you!" attitude prompted me into action. We paraded up and down the street, banging our instruments, until finally that Jewish neighbor—Mrs. Goldberg—realized what had happened and rushed into the street to reclaim her now-contaminated possessions. At the time, I was only sorry because my mother gave me a good pounding for that escapade; it was only later that I realized the enormity and insolence of my "parade."

As I said, I was a brat. I couldn't resist the urge to put people in their places (as I saw it). Like a loud mouth neighbor up the street who bought a new Buick and spent days telling everyone how great a car it was, and what features it offered. I felt it was bragging about something quite ordinary (after all, by that time we had a new Packard each year!). So, I used a long carpenter's nail to scratch "100 TIN" across the car body in big enough letters for everyone to see. I caught hell again for that, and I suspect it cost my father some money. My parents had little patience for my antics, and reprimanded me continually. However, from time to time they would have their hands full with other worries.

CHAPTER 2

Secret Passageways

Apparently impressed by Ben's growing signs of wealth a local hood, a minor-league Mafia wannabe named Little Augie, found himself a little strapped for funds. So, he kidnapped my father—just grabbed him out of his candy store on Myrtle Avenue one day in broad daylight. They drove around Brooklyn for as long as it took to convince Ben that he should give up the contents of the cash register. It was a hard sell though because Ben could be quite stubborn. Augie smashed him across the cheek with his pistol at one point, leaving a scar that Ben carried until the day he died. After a few hours, Ben was finally "convinced." They stopped at the store; my father went in, emptied the register and gave him the cash and Little Augie drove off.

Ben never tried to get even, but my mother took it personally. She anonymously called Little Augie inviting him to a movie theater lobby for a "good time." After he was there a short time, the police took him in for questioning based on a tip they received about a pimp and panderer who was supposedly in the movie lobby looking for underage kids. Augie spent some time in the precinct house wriggling out of that one: he never realized he had been set up. I said he was a hood, not that he was bright!

A month later he sauntered into the candy store when my mother was there alone. When she saw who it was, she didn't hesitate. She reached for a heavy frying pan that she kept handy to repel the unwanted, and "wham," banged him over the head. He was out cold when she dragged him out onto Myrtle Avenue and laid him across the trolley tracks. Fortunately, for him, he woke up before the trolley came, but he never bothered our family again. This was my first exposure to a mob-type of character. I never imagined that some day I'd get an even closer and longer look.

Academically, I was mostly an "A" student, excelling in everything except arithmetic. My arithmetic teacher, Mr. Katz, always referred to me as "four

14

eyes." He wouldn't hesitate to say, "four eyes," come to the front of the room, which understandably made me self-conscious. I would scrunch behind my desk each day to avoid his line of sight in hopes that he would forget all about me. This might account for my poor test results in his class. In the other classes I was a good student, though I wasn't the teacher's pet.

I had a mean streak of my own, and Edward Fink, who sat directly in front of me, was my regular victim. I'd load up my pen with ink from the inkwell on my desk—that's what we had in those days, ink wells with nibs you changed every so often—and then I would spatter ink on the back of his shirt. Hey, I was conducting Rorschach testing, before I even knew what Rorschach testing was. I'd blow bubbles with my chewing gum and explode them onto his hair. And I told all the kids that Edward had potatoes in his ear—which was an expression we had about someone who didn't have clean ears: they had so much dirt in them potatoes could grow.

All year the kids kept looking in his ears, which must have annoyed him to no end. In short I made his life miserable. Obviously he told his parents, because immediately after one of my more outrageous assaults, my mother was asked to visit the school principal. I presume this resulted in "some" change in my attitude, but of course I only remember the fun. When things got dull in class, at least dull to me, I'd break the skin of an orange, squeeze it a little and wait. The sweet smell would move through the classroom, prompting the teacher to go hunting for the origin of the smell, never failing to get the kids giggling. I loved this gag, though I could only do it a few times a year, without giving myself away.

Being a ringleader at school, I was often given special jobs like class monitor, which I imagine was intended to redirect my mischief-making energy into more useful directions. It didn't work out quite like they had planned. I would order the kids around, making them wait for no reason, or commanding them to walk a chalk line or some other silly thing. For the most part they went along with me laughing over the ridiculous things that I would have them do. But I created bottlenecks, if not disorder, in the hallways and I soon lost my school monitor armband. I guess I just wasn't cut out to be part of the establishment.

Most of these escapades took place in grammar school, and I outgrew many of them when I entered high school, where my excess energy finally found its natural channel: organized sports and competition. I had always excelled at street games like hopscotch and jump rope (I was a champion at double and triple Dutch-jumping). There wasn't a kids' game I couldn't master. Jacks, card games, board games, whatever—I was the champ. Organized sports merely heightened my competitive instinct. I loved to win and had plenty of opportunities at the Public School Athletic League events with foot races and games, and I took part in all of them.

But, after school, when we weren't "doing" something, we would "watch" the commerce of the street, which was so different from today's automated world. In my day there was the iceman, a rubber blanket over one shoulder, picking up huge cakes of ice with his tongs. He would lug them into our kitchens and then place them into our iceboxes to keep the food cold. So much is taken for granted today, like the simplicity of the refrigerator. On those summer days when it was hot, we'd wait until he was inside a building, then we'd scrape shavings from the cakes of ice in his truck, getting as many into our mouths as we could before the man returned. The milkman, carrying his bottles in heavy wire baskets door to door and the knife sharpener, in his cart with the hand-driven-grinding wheel were frequent visitors on the block. For amusement, everyone loved the organ grinder with his little monkey. People inside their homes would hear the music and come to the window to throw out coins wrapped in newspaper, then watch the monkey scramble to retrieve the little packages and tip his hat. Similar to today, we also had newspaper delivery boys, and my favorite: the ice cream truck. It was my favorite as long as I wasn't denied an ice cream bar as punishment for some outrageous behavior.

My mother, though devoted to us, worked constantly with my father, and he was increasingly interested only in money and what it could buy. So, in a sense we had to create our own life on the block. Our two-story house was large, with a finished basement, a garage, a large lawn, and a backyard—which my mother had paved because she didn't like dirt of any kind. In the warmer months we had beautiful garden furniture, complete with umbrellas and canopies so that we could relax outdoors. In the winter the furniture was stored so we could flood the backyard for ice-skating. It could be considered a rather normal house except for the fact that my father was a collector of the unusual. For a while we housed two colorful macaws—birds that were large, exotic and sometimes loud. They would sing and squawk in their cages, which were hung out on our clothesline. If the birds weren't exotic enough, Ben next brought home an Alligator. It was cute and kept in a tank in the backyard until it was full-grown, and then it wasn't so cute and adorable anymore.

We had to give it a wide berth, because it could snap your leg off if it caught you. I never did understand how and why he got the creature. Perhaps he thought it was a good watchdog. My mother didn't like it either and was after Ben to get rid of it constantly. She had a good case because she had to feed the thing, and it frightened her to be shoving meat on the end of a stick toward an alligator with its jaws wide open. As news of our "watchdog" spread, more and more people would come to see for themselves. The last straw was when men in a dump truck pulled into our driveway, intending to see the roadside attraction. They cracked all the concrete and my mother blew up. So, finally, Ben disposed of the alligator. He didn't say where. We didn't ask.

But, this was all part of Ben's continued drive to accumulate things. It consumed more and more of his time, leaving little for his family. By 1930 he had a prosperous radio store chain and was mentioned in the newspapers as the "King of Radio Stores." A millionaire by the time he was 35 years old, he owned the second largest radio store chain in the East, consisting of 14 stores and 20 trucks, generating $3.25 million in annual business. This lasted until 1932, when Brooklyn Radio closed, like so many other businesses during the depression. But we never went without. Ben joined another retailer to form Smith-Benny Sales Company to market appliances. My father believed in keeping money in circulation, you might say.

I missed the old candy store neighborhood. But I created a busy life in this new one, partly because my youngest sister Terri was too young to play with, and my older sister bored me. I was only nine when one afternoon Needy and I were sent to the movies, and when we came back, there she was, my baby sister. My mother gave birth to her in the house—but this time on purpose! So with my mother now occupied with a new infant, and Needy and I being competitive we tried to outdo each other often, like seeing who could manufacture the most exaggerated stories. Sometimes I got in over my head.

My Aunt Leon Tene—my mother's sister—lived across the street with her Italian husband, Max Scaffidi. It was the time of the "Red Scare," and the Sacco-Vanzetti trial (those hapless, harmless immigrants accused of a murder and reviled for their supposed hatching of a communist plot to plant a bomb in the New York Stock Exchange) who were scheduled to be executed on August 22, 1927, after a lengthy six-year trial. There were all these wild rumors of a "Sacco-Vanzetti gang" still functioning in New York, although, no hard evidence of this gang ever emerged. But, spurred on by this, I began to tell everybody that my aunt's husband Max, was a member of this "gang."

As in all neighborhoods, rumor traveled fast and out of the blue I was invited to take free "elocution lessons" from Mrs. Campbell, a nosy neighbor in her house nearby. A short time later my mother found an FBI agent at the door inquiring about her brother-in-law. It didn't take long for her to figure out what had happened and who was behind it. Did I ever catch hell over that! I was grounded for a while, and had to apologize to everybody. The only reason I didn't suffer more was because I really didn't realize the effect of what I had done. I never learned that I didn't have the whole picture until after the damage was done. By that time, more often than not, I had embarrassed my mother, enraged neighbors, and gotten myself in deeper trouble.

My mother would often say: "Neddy was born and came out like a flower, and you came out like a snapper turtle!" In later years she would say of her daughters, I had "Faith, hope and Harriet." At the same time she would also say, "Of my three girls, Harriet will go the furthest!" High school distracted me from mischief—for a while—and I was popular enough to be accepted into a sorority. Of course I first had to prove myself through an initiation that had me push a peanut—with my nose—ten blocks along Avenue "J" at midday, while all the people laughed at me. I laughed too. There were many social events with schoolmates, as well as the Friday nights in Meyers Ice Cream Parlor, where we stuffed ourselves on banana splits and gossiped about boys and the teachers we had. Those were great years.

When I enrolled at James Madison High School I was already known as an athlete. But just as my mother thought I was settling down I quickly acquired a reputation for pranks and mischief. So much so that she had to enroll me in an all-girls school, *Girls Commercial* on Eastern Parkway near Prospect Park, to head off expulsion. Once away from all those other kids, especially the boys, I did settle down enough to do well (after all, I was smart and could be a good student once I lost the big audience to perform for).

Family life might not have been close during this period, but it certainly was lively. Ben loved to entertain and show off his well-furnished house. In the basement, the piece de resistance was a giant $4500 pool table with ivory inlays and an automatic ball-return (called a subway because the balls once pocketed rolled through under-the-table channels to one end of the table). We liked to demonstrate this feature to the other kids, and before long, we all became pretty good pool players. Needy preferred the pool table for necking with her boyfriends; I found a place to watch undetected. She also liked to neck on the swing placed in our (paved) backyard. I liked this spot too because I could sprinkle them with hot water while they were occupied with one another, and then watch them jump. In some ways, this exemplified our relationship—she was sentimental and "normal," while I was lively and unconventional.

As fascinating as I thought our own house was, the one next door was even more mysterious, and afforded another glimpse of illicit life. Living there was a bootlegger and—in my own mind anyway—a counterfeiter. Since I was a kid during prohibition I knew all the stories about speakeasies and bootleggers. Everyone knew at least one bootlegger and some private "nightclub" where liquor was available. I had an easy entrée to this one, because it was the home of my best friend Barbara Brauston. Her father Barney ran the bootlegging business with homing pigeons, which drove my mother crazy. Not the bootleg-ging—the pigeons! He would use them to communicate with his suppliers, a nearly foolproof method that was almost as fast as the telephone. My mother would argue with Barney because the pigeons were messy and a health hazard. She'd have to hose down the sidewalks and house windows regularly, because of pigeon dirt. She'd yell at Barney about it, but he'd wave her off.

She'd call the Board of Health, who upon inspecting, agreed with my mother and ordered Barney to get rid of the pigeons. He did, but before long he'd have a new batch, just as dirty and omnipresent as the previous ones and my mother would be on the phone yelling at Barney again. He eventually erected a six-foot high iron fence to discourage prying eyes, but that didn't stop me. (It didn't hinder the pigeons, either.) I was convinced there were mysteries to be solved and adventures awaiting me in that house. Picking times when the adults weren't home, and sometimes with Barbara as my guide, I would climb over the fence and sneak inside.

It was three stories high, with a laundry chute that ran from the top floor to the basement. I loved sliding down that chute, with its turns and steep incline, only to land with a soft plop in the laundry basket next to the washing machine in the basement. There was a small secret room there, behind a false wall you opened with a hairpin—according to Barbara—that housed printing materials and equipment. In my romantic imagination this was enough to make Barney a counterfeiter, perhaps in some foreign currency I thought. Or maybe it was some official-looking papers or something, where the printing didn't have to be that precise.

I told my parents about this great mystery, but they weren't interested. Whether they didn't believe it, or didn't want to get involved, I don't know. It sure fascinated me, though, and I couldn't understand why Barbara didn't try and get the whole story. For now, these were adult mysteries beyond my reach.

CHAPTER 3

That Long Weekend

Like my sister Needy, wrestling with her boyfriends on our pool table in the basement, I too had my boyfriend—and my standards, which were much less flagrant than my sisters. My steady boyfriend was Harold Abrams, the son of an English family in the neighborhood. We went to school together and liked each other at first sight. I spent more time with him than any other boy, although, I did date others from time to time. We continued to see each other after Harold graduated from high school and then began to go steady. He got a job as a circulation manager for the Brooklyn Eagle, our borough newspaper. Looking back on our relationship from a distance of 50 years, I'm surprised to find that I can scarcely remember him. Though I do recall that he washed hundreds of windows to pay for a watch and an ankle bracelet that I still wear today.

At the time he seemed like my intended future, or at least that's what we persuaded ourselves was the case. Though he was just past his teens, we began to talk about marriage, which outraged my opinionated mother. She was backing another of my beaus, Ernie Rosemarin who seemed to her, as an engineer, to have better prospects. (In a strange episode of reverse snobbery, Ernie's mother had forbidden him to come to the house because my mother was Irish!). But at this point in my life, I felt like I had the world by the tail. I had graduated from school, I had a boyfriend, and I had independence and security; because Needy and I had started our own business, designing and selling hats, in what would be the first of my many encounters and involvements in the fashion industry. (Later I would go on to the McDowell Fashion Institute.)

Taking over the breakfast room in our house with our mother's active help, we created hats of our own design, and all the young people in our neighborhood (now high school graduates starting full-time work) came to see and buy. I'd go once a week to the Mecca of the garment district on 38th Street between Fifth and Sixth Avenues in Manhattan, to pick out what material we wanted, and also have them "block" the felt—the first stage in hat design. Back in Brooklyn, we'd embellish them with ribbons, feathers, and other trimmings to make them stylish.

At a time when a good hat cost $25 and up (a large sum in those days), we were selling chic one-of-a-kind creations for $10 and $15, earning about $100 a week. Most of it was profit too, because we had no outside labor costs, no rent and no taxes. Hats, especially stylish ones such as we could produce, were always in fashion in those days and a real necessity for the single girl looking to impress. I am reminded of this period of my life every time I open my closet, because many years later I would again make hats (as a hobby only!) and my walls are lined with rhinestone baseball caps and other evidence of my slightly outrageous imagination.

Our business only lasted for about a year. By then Needy and I were arguing more frequently, and finally she got married to her longtime boyfriend and they moved to upper Manhattan. Girls in those days weren't really encouraged to be serious about business. So, with Needy gone and I only in my late teens not wanting to go it alone, the business was abandoned. But what I had learned from it would come in handy later in life. I didn't miss the hat business because along with Harold, I had something else to hold my attention: a passion for swimming.

Throughout all this activity (my hat business, swimming routine, and Needy's move out of the house), Harold, over my mother's continued objection, was still a major part of my life. When I finally got tired of hearing my mother list all the reasons why Harold was no good for me, I did what any defiant young girl would do. In the autumn of 1936, on a brisk October day, I grabbed Harold, took him to City Hall and married him. Needy was my witness. My mother had secretly gotten married when she was very young, so I don't know why she was so surprised.

Her father was a very strict Catholic man. She and her two sisters would wait until after he did the rounds with his flashlight to see that all the kids were asleep, then put mannequins (the type of dummy's used to pattern clothes) in their beds, and sneak out to the dance halls, where she ultimately met Ben. But it was an entire year later before my Aunt Pauline let the cat of the bag. "Is this true?" her father asked, "Are you married? He demanded that she bring the man to the house to meet the family. She did, and after meeting Ben, she was told that she would have to move out immediately. "A married woman should live with her husband."

So, I got married and my mother went through the roof. "You spoiled your life, ruined your chance to be somebody." I figured the only plans I had ruined were hers, and I was determined to stay married to Harold. Like so many girls of my generation, marriage for me was kind of make believe, fun, and exciting. Something you did because everyone was doing it. We honeymooned at the Waldorf-Astoria Hotel in New York City and for three days sat on the bed eating Ebinger cakes (a brand from a popular Brooklyn bakery), ice cream and listening to the radio. Eventually, we did get to the sex part of it, but we were still like two kids on a lark. We were playing at being grownups, though somehow we knew (at least I knew) that it would eventually end. And indeed, it did, but, not for another four months. We got a one-room apartment not too far from my mother's house and had a great time furnishing it. Once a week on payday we'd go and buy something: only the best Stroheim & Rohman decorator fabrics, Duncan Phyfe couch, and oil paintings for the wall.

I loved the shopping but other than that there was nothing in my life to keep me connected to Harold. I had married him to be married (in those days 20 was an old maid) but I was starting to realize that there was another world out there for me, one that did not involve Ocean Avenue and a baby carriage. Harold, a dedicated newspaper man, already knew the shape of the life he wanted—mine was still waiting for me, and it was waiting some place else! So pretty quickly I realized that as much as I hated to admit it, my mother was right, at least about my future with Harold if not about Harold himself (at one point she declared that he would become a compulsive gambler).

Finally, in what now seems like a very unfair move, we hired a truck and emptied the one-room apartment while Harold was at work. We left him with a mattress and a roll of toilet paper. It seemed funny at the time, but now it seems awful. Harold, of course, was livid when he came home to an empty apartment that evening. He screamed at me over the phone. I was a little frightened, but what could he do? As it happened, he did what we expected—nothing. My mother made arrangements for us to move to Miami Beach for 90 days to establish residency for the purposes of me getting a quick and legal divorce. Despite his anger at our highhanded treatment, I think both Harold and I knew we were both too young to begin a real life together, and then by the time we were mature, we had already moved too far apart.

I met him many decades later, and he said to me, "If it weren't for your mother, we would have stayed married." There was a time I might have agreed with him, but then, at this years-after-the-event meeting, I could only say, "Harold, you can't go by that." He eventually ran the circulation department of the Newark Star-Ledger, a big daily newspaper in New Jersey. He was a sweet, gentle guy with only one thing against him: my mother indeed didn't like him. She thought I could do better—and it has to be said, I did. When I saw him he was ill. He said that the first birthday that came and went without word from him meant he was dead. I never heard from him again.

Except for some crying and complaining, I may have not fought the divorce, perhaps, because I was testing my mother to see if she still cared about me. Maybe, I eloped not merely to spite her, but to see what she'd do about it. Naturally, I wouldn't admit those thoughts at the time. The marriage was over but this episode marked a milestone in my life: I was no longer a virgin, and in my eyes that made me an adult. It's just as well my mother acted to pull Harold and me apart though. Otherwise, a lot of wonderful things might never have happened to me.

The summer of 1937 wasn't one of those wonderful things. I was to receive another dose of life's harsh realities, and it seemed more significant than my brief marriage to Harold. My mother suggested a trip to Atlantic City. You'd think she was always an angry mother, using a cat-&-nine-tail switch across the back of my legs as often as she did. Having an overactive kid and an unpredictable husband can make you appear crazier than many other people. In calmer moments—and there were a lot of them, especially as I gained maturity—I realized how smart and talented my mother was. She also had style: not an acquired skill, it's something you have or you don't. Had she been my age, what a pair we would have made. She was a remarkable woman, something that became clearer to me with each new day.

I never could figure out what she saw in Ben, and it was on that trip that we talked about it. At some point, I guess she asked herself the same question. There we were just the two of us, playing tourists on the Jersey shore, strolling the famous Boardwalk; inhaling the fragrance of hot roasted nuts and the fresh sea air. We saw the steel pier, the rolling chairs and other attractions, but despite all the sightseeing my mother had something to tell me. It was at lunch that she explained that in the early days of their marriage, my mother and Ben weren't home together much. They took turns manning the candy store, and in his off-hours, Ben (as I said earlier) liked to go out with the boys, often staying out all night. My mother grew lonely, and in a movie theater one evening, met a man, an Irishman, named Moury Reilly, who was nice to her. They became friends, then lovers. It was then that she became pregnant with me.

But, in the midst of secret plans to get divorced from Ben so she could marry her true love, he fell victim to the 1918 tuberculosis epidemic that ravaged New York and other cities, and died. It was a crushing blow to her. Her mother had been advising her against seeking a divorce—Ben would fight it, and with all his money, he would probably win. Besides, my grandmother told her, why run away from all that money and into a world of certain poverty, especially now that the man you want to marry is dead? So my mother agreed that she had no other choice. She said nothing to Ben and carried on in the marriage as though nothing had changed. It took a moment for the words to sink in, for me to understand what I was hearing. I was confused by this news. "Ben is not my father?" I asked. I didn't know how to feel. I didn't particularly like Ben, or feel any closeness with him. Still, he was the only father I knew.

"No, he is not your father. Morey O'Reilly was your father," she said softly, emotion on her face. And I needed you to know that before…" The words were echoing in my head, like bullets from a Tommie gun ricocheting off all the walls of my brain. There were so many thoughts, and they were all so loud that I couldn't seem to interpret any of them. After a short hesitation, "Before what?" I asked. "Before…before…I die. I have cancer Harriet, and they don't know how long I have.

My whole life I had been a prankster, a troublemaker, an attention getter and to some degree a bit of a brat. At this moment, I felt—maybe for the first time—like an adult, and I didn't like it, not one bit. From then on I knew I was soon to be on my own. My mother, my biggest champion, had her days numbered (she would live two more years, until New Year's eve 1939–40, but didn't know that then). My sister Needy and I never saw eye to eye on anything, and never would, especially now that she and her husband Arty had moved to California. My little sister Terri was too young to count on for anything, and Ben was always there, of course, but he wasn't someone I confided in regularly because he didn't seem to invite it. He and I would never be that close except perhaps, in his last few years when he had few others to talk to or visit with, and was becoming senile. I eventually told Ben about my real father, but I waited until the 1950's when my mother was long gone, and we were both too old to shock anymore. Even then, he broke down and cried.

That weekend long ago in Atlantic City with my mother was my first introduction to a real life crisis, rather than the simple imitation of one that I experienced earlier in life. I never realized then that I was on a road to a very different, more exciting, and I believe more fulfilling life than my mother ever experienced. As it was, she could only play the hand she was dealt. I always thought she deserved better than that. At that time I thought the future looked grim.

I was choked up. I didn't know what to say, or how to say it. We sat there looking out onto the blue Atlantic Ocean. Subconsciously we both knew that conversation, at this moment, was unnecessary. So, we just sat, in the silence, and shared the same space. What more was there to do?

CHAPTER 4

Event of The Century

To most people, in their mind's eye, New York City means skyscrapers, pavement, and noise—not water. Did you know that it is surrounded by water? Most people don't. In fact, four of New York City's five boroughs are islands, which means that the Atlantic Ocean is always at our door. The beaches were our escape hatches from urban swelter. From most anywhere in Brooklyn, it was a short hop to the beach. For many of us without a car—or someone to drive us—there was public transportation: buses and the subway. Almost all the Brooklyn-bound subways terminated a short walk from some beach. I would take the BMT to Coney Island and then the eastbound bus past Brighton and Manhattan Beaches to Oriental Beach—the nicest one along that stretch. It no longer exists today; the oceanfront property became a part of Kingsborough College in the 1960's.

But in my day Oriental Beach was the only private beach in that area. By private I mean you had to pay to use the lockers, showers, the pool and the beach itself. Some people would walk around onto the beach from the ocean side of Manhattan Beach, without paying, and lie on the sand and enjoy the surf—but they weren't supposed to do so. At times the lifeguards chased them off. I liked Oriental Beach mostly because I could do what I liked to do more than anything else: swim laps in its giant pool. My membership cost $25.00 per year, can you imagine?

I began to take swimming seriously when I finished school in the spring of 1934. Because our family had money, there wasn't pressure on me to go to work to support myself. Instead, I was busy with my little experiments in adulthood: my short-lived business with Needy and short lived-marriage to Harold. I spent my summer months doing lap after lap, day after day, building up my stamina. I knew I wanted to compete, but as it turned out it was show business I was in training for, though I didn't know it at the time. One morning, as I was completing my daily swim an older man, tall and thin with graying hair, approached me and introduced himself as Bill Merriam, a swimming coach from the University of Pennsylvania. He was recruiting swimmers for the Olympics of 1936 and said he would coach me for the try-outs if I would practice everyday.

I loved the idea. So I arrived each morning at 7:30 a.m. and swam laps under the watchful eye of coach Merriam. He kept track with a stopwatch, and could blend the personalities of drill sergeant and cheerleader to get the most of my efforts. In three months I could feel I was getting faster and stronger, and was eager to be tested. But one morning he failed to show up. The next day, again no coach, and there was no sign of him after that either. A short time later I was told that the newspaper reported that he had died suddenly of a heart attack. Being a kid I didn't know what else to do except forget the whole idea. It never occurred to me to ask around about other Olympic swimming scouts, and the 1936 Olympics came and went without me.

But I continued to swim. In the winter months I'd go to an indoor pool at the St. George Hotel, the nicest hotel in downtown Brooklyn, and the only indoor pool in the borough. Opened in 1929, it was built over a natural salt-water spring that kept the pool filled and was illuminated by elaborate Art Deco fixtures; enclosed by mirrored walls and ceiling—it was like swimming in a museum! Famous people swam there, including Johnny Weismuller and Esther Williams, two people I would get to know later in my life. At that time, however, I didn't know anything about celebrities. I just liked to swim.

At first, I didn't have the same drive and energy without coach Merriam, but I kept doing my crawl, backstroke, and sidestroke, just the way I'd been taught. And maybe I was clairvoyant because in 1938 I saw an ad in the Brooklyn Eagle (Harold's newspaper). The Aquacade, an attraction to be highlighted at the 1939 The World's Fair, less than a year away, was holding tryouts for girl swimmers. The Fair, which was going to be in Flushing Meadows, was heavily publicized as the event of the century, and I knew all about it. I didn't know much about what an Aquacade was, who Billy Rose (the producer) was, or exactly what it needed in the way of swimmers, but I did know I wanted to be part of it.

Tryouts were held at the St. George Hotel. I was so eager to do well that my adrenaline was sky-high when it came my turn to swim. I couldn't wait to the hit the water. My early training by coach Merriam and my conditioning paid off. I breezed through all the trials with lots of energy left, and flashed a big smile. So I wasn't surprised when they called my name. I was to be a member of a company of swimmers that would be backing up the stars, Eleanor Holm and Johnny Weismuller. I had a job!

The World's Fair made New York City the place to be that spring of 1939. All the preparations, its stars, the publicity it generated, all overshadowed much of the news of a pending war in Europe. The Fair was a glorious change of pace for the millions of people who came to see the countless attractions. Millions of dollars were spent creating the various international and U.S. exhibits, the park-like landscape, and the soon-to-be-familiar symbols, the Trylon and the Perisphere. There were well-known restaurants such as Lundy's, Caruso's and Nathan's, as well as small hotdog/waffle booths so the crowds were never far from an opportunity to eat and drink. Remember, this was long before Walt Disney World (or Walt Disney Land for that matter) making the fair an incredible experience.

Crowds came to the amusement area for the parachute jump, with its tall, spidery, silhouette against the sky and its quickly earned reputation as a test of bravery where hundreds of boys (and girls) from out of town tested their mettle. There were lots of other rides, too—the fun of the past with a glimpse of the future. If you followed the looped road around Fountain Lake you'd come to the biggest attraction of the World's Fair, Billy Rose's Aquacade. It was staged nightly in an eleven thousand-seat amphitheater that had been built by the state of New York and leased to Billy Rose for the run of the show.

The show itself was similar to one that Billy had staged at the Fair in Cleveland two years earlier with the same stars, Eleanor Holm and Johnny Weismuller. The show included lots of swimmers, stars, a great orchestra, and some comedians. For the opening, Eleanor Holm and then Johnny would dive into the water in their patented sleek style in front of a 72-foot American flag. Providing the window dressing for these featured acts were the AquaBelles and the AquaBeaux, the AquaGals and the AquaDudes, and the AquaFemmes—all different groups of young men and women swimmers who were featured in different parts of the show.

Each segment had swimming routines choreographed by Eleanor for the girls' water-ballet sequences, and Floyd Zimmerman, who handled the male water movement. Some of our swimsuits were skimpy; some of them bikini-style (called two-piece suits in 1939). Some were flesh-colored, almost see-through, and from the distance of the seats, it probably looked as if we were all naked (in contrast to the belief held by youngsters today that we were all prudes back then). The girls' chorus was divided into two groups: we AquaBelles were the swimmers and the AquaMaids merely stood around on the pool ledge to decorate the stage. As swimmers, we were proud of our status and we looked down on the AquaMaids as lesser talents. But it was all show business, painstakingly planned and practiced to perfection.

The lights would go out after each scene, and sometimes when the next scene opened we would be on the pool's edge ready to dive. Other times, we would already be in the water when the lights came up. Sometimes Eleanor would do long solo bits, with lots of backstroking so that the audience could see her more clearly. Then we would join her, moving in formation and matching her back and front strokes in a coordinated rhythm. What the audience saw represented hours and hours of practice. And then the finale! Remember, this was 1939—1940 and war in Europe was imminent, with high speculation that America would join in. What the spectators got was a rousing George M. Cohan style patriotic songfest entitled "Yankee Doodle's Going to Go to Town Again!" The centerpiece was an American flag, a block long.

All of this entertainment took place in 65 minutes, four times a day, seven days a week. The fair-goers loved it, and the critics raved. Variety called it "a cinch draw," while other quotes included, "Biggest bargain of the World's Fair" (New York Daily Mirror), "a colossal spectacle" (NY Post), "a large and enormous water carnival" (NY Times), "Biggest show on earth" (Daily News). I was dazzled; all of show business was new to me! I was 21 years old and the biggest audience I had ever drawn was when I pushed a peanut down Avenue J with my nose during my high school sorority initiation! It still stuns me, after all these years, that I was part of this historical event. About 11 million people paid 75 cents (the gate fee, which went to the World's Fair Committee to offset costs), plus the cost of a seat (from 40 to 99 cents) to see the show. There was some griping after the fair ended that Billy Rose made so much money. But to his credit, the Aquacade also paid more gate fees than any other attraction.

It's difficult now to describe how much of an impact the Aquacade had on the World's Fair, unless you knew something about its creator. Billy Rose was an impresario, Broadway producer, writer, nightclub owner, columnist, songwriter, humorist, philanthropist, publicity hound, ladies' man, and the guy with the biggest ego on the Great White Way. He liked two things: making money and having his name spelled right in the newspaper. He was successful at both, even though in later years there were some stories he would have preferred the columnists overlooked. When he ran his Times Square nightclub, the Diamond Horseshoe, he wrote all the advertising himself. He had a flair for attracting patrons with money. His writing was so colorful and irresistible that he was invited to write his own newspaper column about show biz, "Pitching Horseshoes," for the NY Daily Mirror. Although Billy was successful as a stockbroker/financier, he was soon attracted by the glamour of show biz. So, he turned his energy to attracting customers for his entertainment rather than his stock tips. In his early Wall Street years, he had a truly wise mentor, financier and world guru, Bernard Baruch, for whom he had done secretarial work.

But Billy achieved recognition on his own and his name came to mean New York glamour, entertainment, and excitement. By the late 1930's he had many well known literary and show biz friends, plus a battery of good lawyers he could call upon, and some other friends in high government places. That's a lot of build up for a guy who was only 5'3"! But, what he lacked in height he made up for in brass and charm.

His campaign to win the World's Fair contract was among his greatest achievements as a promoter and showman. According to Billy's biographer, his contract to lease space at the World's Fair was complex, and negotiated to Billy's advantage. Initially he sought the positions of either director of entertainment or director of concessions. However, both positions had already been named when he first inquired in 1937, and so he was then determined to stage his Aquacade instead, and he did. But despite his successful reputation, we knew him only as someone who exploited the reputations (both professional and personal) of his stars.

Billy lured Johnny Wiessmuller away from MGM by promising him the same salary he had in Hollywood, knowing that his Hollywood background and recognition value would give added star-power to the Aquacade—not to mention his flashy, photographic face! For all of you too young to know, Johnny Weissmuller was the original Tarzan for all those films of the '30's and '40's, as well as the Jungle Jim serials that followed. And before Hollywood, Johnny was an Olympic gold medallist.

Eleanor Holm (who was Billy's wife during the Aquacade) also had a show business background with its roots, like Johnny's, in the Olympics. She was a backstroke championship when she was only 14, had tallied 29 AAU championships, and by the time she won her first gold medal at the 1932 Olympics in Los Angeles, she had six world records. Her Hollywood career however only materialized after the tremendous publicity generated when she was sensationally kicked off the 1936 Olympic Team—before she had an opportunity to compete.

Weismuller & Holm

Eleanor was aboard the S.S. Manhattan as a member of the U.S. Olympic squad (the first woman to ever make three Olympic teams) headed to Germany to compete in Hitler's backyard. Many people other than athletes were aboard the ship, including famed newspaper writer Charlie MacArthur—husband of Helen Hayes and coauthor of the play "Front Page." Late one evening Eleanor left the lower level berths assigned to the athletes to go to first class and crack open a bottle of champagne—maybe more than one—with Charley and others. He woke up with a hangover the next morning and faced the wrath of Helen, while Eleanor, whose devil-may-care reputation already had made her famous on board, faced the wrath of Avery Brundage, the U.S. Olympic team czar, who promptly kicked her off the team without a second thought.

She protested, "The regulations stated that all team members should continue the same training preparations that we were accustomed to having in the States. That's all I was doing." This was indeed true and despite the irregularity of her "training routine," she hadn't lost a meet in seven consecutive years! But, Brundage didn't want to hear it. In Berlin, Eleanor could only watch as a Dutch woman went on to win the backstroke gold metal with a rather tepid pace. "I could have won with a glass of champagne in one hand, a bottle in the other," she was quoted as saying afterward.

Many years later Eleanor would credit Avery Brundage for making her a household name. Without him, she said, "I would have just been another swimmer." The resulting publicity about her escapades was called to Billy's attention. They dated then married. He came to realize that someone as beautiful and as fabled as she was would be a sensation, and shortly thereafter staged the first Aquacade in Cleveland Ohio with Eleanor as the star. His timing (or luck) was perfect.

CHAPTER 5

It's Who You Sleep With

Of course, even with the stars secure, all was not smooth sailing. For a moment it appeared that the Aquacade of 1939 would not open as scheduled. A grueling rehearsal schedule (for which we weren't paid!) meant that all the girls began getting colds, flu and were too sick to rehearse or perform. We complained about a rule that said sick or not you got fined if you missed either. We felt that was unfair, so we griped about it. Nothing happened until Eleanor took up our case with Billy, and when he didn't show any sign of relenting, she took it to the health authorities. Then the American Federation of Actors union got involved and a strike seemed inevitable. Billy was ripping mad—he was a hot head much of the time those days anyway, and Eleanor really knew how to push his buttons. So to make the unions go away and make Eleanor happy, Billy had to inaugurate a new provision that provided for rehearsal time pay and a clause that said you couldn't be docked if you were sick. But it didn't end there. Billy had other ways of holding down expenses.

To make up for what happened he created a list of regulations that we had to adhere to; one of which stated that any performers caught holding hands or otherwise showing affection would be fined $5 per incident. Most of us were kids, always having a crush on someone or other, and being in these confined circumstances and parading around in bathing suits, romances were inevitable. Even simple signs of affection, like a goodbye kiss or a pat on the shoulder would trigger a fine. (Billy was everywhere! Nothing got by him when he or his spies were on the prowl). Somehow, despite all the backstage drama, the show did go on. And even with all the alternative entertainment competition in and around New York City, the Aquacade attracted almost eight—of the forty-seven—million people that attended the World's Fair, better than any other attraction there.

In addition to his show business triumphs, Billy was known for his magnificent collections, sculptures among them. He collected lots of things, including wives. He had five, beginning with Fanny Brice, the ethnic Jewish actress and comedian, who starred in the Ziegfield Follies during the 1920s and 1930s. She became known for her beautiful voice and limber grace, which she always used in the service of humor. She made such songs as "My Man," and "Second Hand Rose," famous, and was paid tribute by Barbra Streisand in the loosely biographic film "Funny Girl," in the 1960s.

Fanny's marriage to Billy failed, along with her Hollywood film career as she attempted to shed her comedic roots for serious drama. Regardless, Fanny was a huge presence and later found success in radio. Her baby Snooks character was loosely reborn in Lily Tomplin's Edith Ann character, many decades later. It was Billy who filed for divorce in 1939, because he believed that he would always be known as "Mr." Fanny Brice. And, Billy never played second fiddle.

His next bride was inevitably Eleanor Holm, a free spirit if there ever was one and as sharp-tongued on the comeback as Billy. He divorced Eleanor in 1952, but not before some public squabbling over money, and then married Joyce Matthews (he would marry her twice, just as Milton Berle did). He also married Doris Warner Vidor, from one of the prominent Hollywood families. All his marriages ended in divorce, and the stories behind them were almost as sensational as the Aquacade Extravaganzas!

Of these women, I only knew one: Eleanor Holm, because I swam with her in the Aquacade, and spent a lot of time with her between shows. She was as beautiful as Billy's publicity proclaimed, as well as being spirited, enthusiastic and witty. A natural, beautiful swimmer, she was the hit of the show, despite the presence of Johnny Weismuller and later Buster Crabbe, and the somewhat beyond her prime Gertrude Ederle; the much heralded English Channel swimmer. Florenz Ziegfeld, of the Ziegfeld Follies said that Eleanor had "the most beautiful figure I have ever seen." She was also a genuinely nice person.

Along with headlining the show, Eleanor had to carry the burden of her problem with alcohol (something the biographies of showman Rose never mentioned) and a marriage to a roving-eye husband always surrounded by beautiful women. She was always described as quick-witted, fun loving, and totally dedicated to Billy. This was true until 1951 when he got involved with showgirl Joyce Matthews, in a bizarre drama.

Ironically, it was the Broadway gossip columnists, those skilled writers of show biz doings who people like Billy Rose usually sought out in order to keep their names before the public, who torpedoed Billy's marriage to Eleanor. Celebrities indulging in extracurricular love affairs have never been rarities, and for the most part these rumors never got written about, so the "injured party" was never publicly embarrassed. But, every now and then, a story must have seemed irresistible and this was one of those stories.

Joyce Matthews was well known to the show biz set. Beautiful, vivacious, flaky, but not especially talented, she set her sights on Billy and zeroed in. Billy was never shy when it came to women, but was usually careful not to be seen with them in public places. This time he wasn't and Earl Wilson, among the best-known Broadway columnists, in July 1951, reported that Billy and Joyce were sharing a hotel room in Canada for the weekend. Everybody in New York saw the item; including Eleanor, who had been told that Billy was checking out some oil deal that Bernard Baruch had told him about. When a reporter queried her, Eleanor said of Billy, "He can't be that dumb." As it turned out, he was.

Billy and Joyce, having seen the item in the paper, knew that scandal was brewing and returned to New York City on Sunday night to Billy's apartment above the Ziegfeld Theater. A huge argument developed when Billy wanted to break off the relationship. Joyce got frantic and threatened to slash her wrists if he left her. She demanded that Billy divorce Eleanor immediately and marry her. Billy hemmed and hawed, pleading for time. When it sounded as if the answer was going to be, "no" Joyce surprised him by picking up a handful of razor blades and cutting herself, spraying blood everywhere. Billy wrest them from her, and she then attempted to jump out of the window. She was wild and out of control and that's when Billy called the police for help. Shortly after, all those in the English-speaking world who hadn't heard about the romance were now filled in authoritatively by police reports to the press.

Eleanor didn't give Billy much chance to explain and quickly filed for divorce. Her lawyer was the famous Louis Nizer, who occasionally took time off from social reform to become a high-priced divorce expert. When Eleanor wouldn't listen to "reason," (according to Billy) and divorce was imminent, Billy sought in vain to limit his responsibilities to a small annual alimony fee, and began spreading rumors about her. Every smear, everything about her that would taint her character, found its way into print. The columnists loved it. They called it the War of the Roses—long before the movie of the same name (starring Michael Douglas and Kathleen Turner.) It went on until the fall of 1952. By then, every hint of a flaw in Eleanor's person, her lovers, past and present, real or imagined, was public knowledge.

Eleanor pulled her life together in time to counter-attack Billy's smear campaign, by embarking on a publicity tour to meet her fans. It was a success and public opinion was definitely on her side in September 1952, when the divorce trial began in New York. Louis Nizer stated her demands: a stiff financial settlement ($200,000 tax free), a yearly $30,000 annuity, and reimbursement for all her legal fees. Billy caved in and Eleanor had the last laugh. What rankled him most was not the money so much—Billy was a multimillionaire by now—but the humiliation. He was seen as a loser in the ordeal, and Billy hated to lose.

Buck Dawson, founder of the International Swimming Hall of Fame, was quoted many years later as stating that Eleanor told him that the Aquacades were her idea, the marriage was Billy's. "My idea was better than his," she said. When she died in 2004 (she was 91) Fred Grimm of the Miami Herald wrote, "All outrageous, whimsical, independent, unconventional, uncompromising, champagne-loving women everywhere should drink a toast to Eleanor."

Of course the marriage scandal between Billy and Eleanor was well after the Aquacade of 1939. During the run of the Aquacade there were other tumultuous dramas being played out, but they were all behind the scenes. The public saw only glamorous perfection. Eleanor was with the Aquacade for its entire run, a good match in style for the dashing Weissmuller. When Johnny was with the show, one of the highlights was the scene where he chased Eleanor around the tank, the two of them, graceful and swift, cavorting like dolphins, while the crowd roared its approval.

We missed Johnny when he departed in early 1940, before the official closing of the fair, because he was nice to us. Not just courteous and helpful, he was solicitous. When one of the AquaBelles got tuberculosis and had no money for doctors (you can imagine Billy Rose didn't have a medical plan for his talent), Johnny paid her entire medical bill. He didn't tell anybody, or make a big deal about it—he just did it. We found out about it later. I never did hear a reason why he left the show. Perhaps he just got tired of the routine by then or perhaps—equally as likely—it had something to do with Billy. Buster Crabbe, Johnny's replacement, was another ex-Olympian with movie credentials. He played Flash Gordon in the TV serials, and a few Tarzan films as well. But, Buster was conceited. He wanted everybody to know who he was and how talented he was. Like Johnny, he was a beautiful swimmer—fast, sleek, and smooth. But in our minds, he couldn't replace Johnny Weismuller, a true champion.

1940 wore on and we knew the Aquacade, along with the rest of the World's Fair, would be coming to an end. Very few of the AquaBelles gave much thought to what would happen next. Most of us were all young kids, believing that being in the Aquacade was just one of those once-in-a-lifetime events; a fun thing we once did. For the most part, we weren't smitten with the show biz bug. We figured we'd go back to our previous lives, which in my case meant back to millinery or a job in some store. That changed without any warning.

Celebrities were always visiting Billy Rose at the Aquacade office, especially those who would be featured performers in the days ahead. When Jimmy Durante strolled through the dressing room we assumed he was there for a social visit, because we knew he wasn't scheduled as a guest star. Like most of the celebrities that visited, Jimmy was friendly, and said "Hi!" to everybody in general before going into Billy's office. We returned to our chitchat. It was late afternoon. We had finished rehearsing and were lounging around before changing into street clothes to go out to eat. (Our schedules were always tight because there rarely was time for a leisurely meal between rehearsals and our 8:30 performance).

I was talking with Eleanor Holm and some other girls when Jimmy was leaving. Spotting Eleanor, an old friend, he came over to say, "hello," and Eleanor introduced us. His first words after "hello," were something like "The Copacabana…that's a new nightclub opening next week, is looking for pretty girls like you." We all nodded and said, "really?" But the experienced (and even the non-experienced) show business girls knew that a new club would interview hundreds of pretty girls and select only a handful. Because of that and the fact that it was opening in less than a week, we were just being polite by acting grateful for Jimmy's advice; it all seemed out of our league.

As he talked with Eleanor he could sense we weren't terribly excited about his news. Suddenly, he looked at me and said, "You, you're a cute number, you're just the type they're looking for. Wouldn't you like to be in the chorus line at the Copacabana?" I flashed him a smile. "Sure, I'd love it." I still wasn't taking this seriously. After all, I might have had a cute face, a terrific figure, and a great smile, but Jimmy wasn't the first guy to pay me complements. However, he was determined to get my attention, and he had a devilish sense of humor. He lowered his voice, "You know, in show business, it's not who you know, it's who you sleep with." Without missing a beat, I said loud enough for everyone to hear, "Well, Jimmy, take your pants off!" I didn't think either of us meant it, but it was the right response: Jimmy howled. He told me where and when to meet him, and that he would show me around the Copa and get me job in the chorus line, and then he left. I didn't really know what being in a chorus line entailed, but I knew it would be more fun than making hats! I could hardly wait. I sensed a magical new chapter in my life was about to begin.

CHAPTER 6

The Age of Glamour

I waited for Jimmy in front of the Copacabana nightclub. I was nervous and excited at the same time. He said he'd get me a job, but still, I was a little skeptical. The club was to open two days from now—November 10—and here I was, a young girl who had never danced in a chorus line before, let alone one in New York City. Still, Jimmy Durante was Jimmy Durante, one of the best-known stars in show business, ready to sponsor me; little Harriet Weber of Brooklyn, all five feet nothing, 105 pounds of me. I was on top of the world, and so I began to imagine it. Jimmy, springing from a cab, interrupted my enticing daydream shouting, "There's my Henrietta!"

From the time we first met that's the name he used for me. He had a nickname for everything. I guess it was his way of making things his own. With me on his arm we climbed the half-dozen steps and opened the heavy door to the brand new supper club. Two days from now, once the club was open for business, a doorman dressed in a tuxedo and top hat would be on hand to open the door and greet the customers. Inside, the waiters, too, would be wearing a tuxedo; as of course did any of the other male employees who came in contact with the public. The image was very upscale.

Once inside, we were in a small foyer. On the left were the offices of the big bosses: Monte Proser, the first owner, and later—beginning in 1943—Jules Podell, the "mobs" man in charge. On the right was the Lounge, which would have been called a bar in any other place but here it was something special. We climbed an elegant flight of stairs to an upstairs foyer, where Jimmy asked to see Jack Entratter, the manager of the day-to-day operations. I was looking around trying to take it all in, trying not to appear as nervous as I was, and trying not to shout out to anybody who could hear: "Hey, look at me! I'm with Jimmy Durante, who's getting me a job in this ritzy New York supper club! How about that!" But I just kept my mouth shut and let Jimmy do the talking.

I was soon introduced to a large man who walked with a slight limp (he had polio as a kid I learned later). After exchanging pleasantries, Jimmy got down to business.

"Jack, here's the girl I told Monte about. Henrietta, meet Jack Entratter, the big man around here. He'll fix you up."

"It's Harriet, Mr. Entratter, nice to meet you," I said.

Jack looked soulfully at Jimmy and shrugged, "Jimmy, we open in two days. All the costumes are done, all the routines rehearsed. Everything's all set."

"C'mon, Jack," Jimmy said, "Do us all a favor, especially Henrietta, who needs a job. She's perfect for this place. Look at the All-American girl-next-door face!" Which of course prompted me to flash my biggest smile.

"But, Jimmy…"

"Jack, I'd really like to see her in the line. C'mon, you can get her ready in time. She's a natural. She was a star at the Aquacade Extravaganza at the World's Fair." After what seemed like a VERY long pause, Jimmy said, "Jack, I'd really like…"

Jimmy's star "capital" apparently was enough, and Jack broke in, "OK, Jimmy. We'll do it. You're right. She's just what we need. What's your name?" Almost shouting from the excitement I said, "Harriet. Harriet Weber, I live in Brooklyn." Turning to Jimmy, he winked, "We can overlook that."

So, just like that, I joined the chorus line at the Copacabana nightclub. Jack and Jimmy said their goodbyes, and I was led backstage where Jack introduced me to Don Loper, the club's costume designer, choreographer and dancer, who needed to outfit me quickly and teach me the routines. My first Copa outfit was a brown-and-orange Harlequin style costume shirred and body hugging, as if you were poured into it—very sexy, yet glamorous. I tried on six-inch wedged shoes, dyed to the match the dress, which fit and added height. Then the famous Copa hat decorated with pineapples and other fruit, feathers and colored ribbons. And lastly, the final touch that gave me that Carmen Miranda look—large round earrings.

From those first moments together Don Loper and I got along famously. He was a prince, especially to me in those early days. Since our opening was only two days from now, and the other girls had already rehearsed, Don rehearsed me then and there (rather than with the show's director, Marjorie). He could see I was willing, but nervous, so he tried to put me at ease. "There are no intricate steps to learn," he said calmly, "Just a few little kicks, a box step and a samba step—like this." And he showed me. Then I tried it. He could see I moved well and caught onto the style and rhythm easily. Once he saw I had a basic grasp of the routine, he stopped me and told me to go home and practice. "Show up early on Saturday," he said, "and we'll go over the routine again."

I raced home. I hadn't told anybody about my tryout because I was afraid something would go wrong, and I didn't want to be embarrassed. But now, I told everyone and anyone I thought I could impress. I was batting a thousand. I had Jimmy Durante and Don Loper on my side. I was determined not to let them down. I practiced a lot in those two days. I even found a pair of six-inch wedgies, so I could get adjusted to my new height. I'm glad I worked as hard as I did, because our before-the-show practice went well, and Don was pleased, therefore so was I. It was the beginning of a long friendship. We would stay in touch long after I was gone from the Copa, and all the while he was in Hollywood in later years, doing costumes design for movies. He was a one-of-a-kind guy.

After the brief run-through with Don before the show, I went downstairs to the Copa dressing room. It was smaller than I had imagined. Tiny almost, considering it was home for six people—now seven including me. For the first time I was nervous about the other girls. I had been so focused on the routine I never considered how they would react to me. Would they accept me? Did I take the place of one of their friends? Would they try to make me look bad? All these thoughts were whirling around in my head.

I was the first one there, but there was no doubt about where I would have to sit. The dressing area consisted of two long back-to-back tables with a large mirror running the length of them. The lights were already turned on. There were six chairs facing six spots before the mirrors, three spots on each side, and each one was "claimed" by combs and other personal items laying on the table-top. I got another chair and made a tiny space at the end of the table nearest the door. I didn't know what to do, so I looked to see if any makeup stuff was there. I pulled open a little drawer looking for something, anything, but there was nothing except for the things already "staked out" on the tables.

Before long, as I was hanging up my clothes, two gorgeous blonde girls came in. They were talking and when they saw me they stopped and gave me a quick look. Then they breezed right by me to their chairs at the opposite table at the other end. Once their coats were hung up, they opened their purses, sat down, and began talking with not a word to me. I didn't know whether to say "hello," or to wait until they were ready to say something. It was awkward. Just then, another girl entered, another blonde just as beautiful as the first two. She started to jabber with the others as if I was invisible. It was obvious that they were snubbing me. Why, I didn't know. Maybe all the new dancers got this treatment. But deep down I knew this wasn't so. For some reason these girls didn't like me; I didn't know why. So I decided to play it cool, mind my business, follow instructions, and do my job.

I wasn't sure just how we were supposed to makeup. I didn't know how a "Copa girl" should look. I'd never been in a nightclub like this, even as a guest let alone back stage. So I sneaked peeks at the other girls and tried to do what they did so I'd look like one of them. When they powdered their noses, so did I. When they applied lipstick and gloss, so did I. When they straightened their stocking seams, so did I. They checked one another to be sure everything was perfect, but no one offered to help me. I had to make do with the mirror. After being in the Aquacade and getting wet four times a day and having to make up so many times, I felt quite confident that I was as good—or better—than most of these girls when it came to using cosmetics. Still, it was unsettling to be cold-shouldered; it seemed to me that camaraderie is what makes a chorus line.

Things remained pretty tense until Don Loper came backstage to see if we were ready. Then it dawned on me. I was so disturbed about being frozen out by the other girls that I had forgotten this was opening night! Everybody was nervous! We were all doing this for the first time. That thought gave me courage. All seven of us were in the room now waiting for our call to go upstairs, spraying on last minute perfume. In a lull in the conversation, I spoke up. "Look, I know I'm new to the line, but I'm here to stay. My name is Harriet Weber and I hope we can be friends." Nothing, they didn't say a word. "Maybe it's just the jitters, but I sense that there's some hostility against me." The silence got heavier. "If I'm wrong, tell me. If there's something else wrong or something bothering you about me, please tell me." Still, silence.

I tried again. "Would you at least tell me your names, since we are going to be dancing together." The silence grew almost unbearable. Without any notice one of the girls with her back to me said, "I'm Bonnie." That broke the ice, and the others spoke up, too. Just then, Don Loper returned, "You're on in two minutes." He pointed at me, and said, "You enter stage right and stay on the top step." This meant I was to follow the other two girls who came on the left, as the audience sees it, and stop at the top of the stage.

How prominent I would be in the line didn't matter much to me then. I was just glad to be there and very eager to go on. I focused on following instructions and remembering what Don had told me during our rehearsals—to watch what the girls on the floor did. Because they were the most experienced, sometimes they liked to do steps not in the routine to make the new dancers look bad he said. I was determined to look terrific. It was just like the moments before my entrance in the Aquacade: my adrenaline was high. We could hear the Master of Ceremonies, Fernando Alvarez, who also served, sometimes, as the bandleader and singer, began the introductions, so we moved into our positions.

There was a flurry of last-minute adjustments, hats, costumes and jewelry. Professional courtesy replaced the hard feelings of moments ago. We all checked one another to see that everything was on right. To the Latin music of Frank Marti and Mike Durso's Samba band, we began our routine to heavy applause. From that very first appearance the Copa girls were a hit, and I never failed to get that rush every time we opened a new show. Despite my nervousness and Don's warning, the other girls never did try to make me look bad. I guess my little speech helped some—that and the fact that it was opening night and everybody wanted everything to be perfect. It was. "I'm a Copa girl! I thought. When's the next show?"

In between shows, customers could dance to the music of the Society Dance bands with either Nat Brandywynne or Ted Stracter wielding the baton. Or, if it was the first show, they could order a meal from the distinctive Copa menu; its cover bearing the soon-to-be-world-famous Copa face and a fruited turban, designed by Wesley Morje of Brazil.

Our schedule called for us to appear twice in each show, once to open and then again after the headliner's performance, to close. Tonight the headliner was Connie Russel. When it was all over we poured into our dressing room happy as kids when school's out. We girls began to talk and my chilly reception, it turns out, was because the other girls thought I was brought in by the mob. I denied that, of course. When asked, I said I had no boyfriend in the Mafia, I didn't know anybody in the Mafia, and I wouldn't even know a Mafiatype it he turned up in my bed! (Boy, was that little speech an omen or something!). I mentioned Jimmy Durante, and while someone muttered something about favoritism and "having pull," our conversation lacked the tension that was in the air earlier.

And just then Jimmy walked in. As blasé as those girls were, someone like that had to impress them. And it did. My stock rose even higher when they heard Jimmy congratulate me and tell me that he was taking me to Reuben's for a bite to eat. I never had any trouble with any of the other Copa girls after the first evening. Over time many of us became friends, and in some cases very good friends. And in many other circumstances, big and small, having Jimmy Durante as a friend boosted my popularity and credibility throughout my stay at the Copa. Because when Jimmy came into the club, he always made time to see me.

While I might remember that first night in 1940 as the terrific premiere of Harriet Weber, show biz regulars remember the date as the debut of the Copacabana, which over the years would provide so much top-drawer talent for New York audiences. But the promise of success was there from the start, beginning with the huge amount of space that that event took up in the entertainment sections of the city's newspapers. The Copa didn't start slowly and build—it was an overnight sensation. Anybody who played there was a celebrity in the columns.

Every columnist, from Winchell to Wilson, covered the opening of each new headliner. A lot of the gossip—"who's doing what to whom," items—were reported as being heard at the Copa, and Monte Proser, Jules Podell, Jack Entratter, Don Loper, and other Copa people became familiar names in the gossip columns. Aside from certain things that were not to be printed (such as the close friendship between Jack Entratter and Mafia kingpins), columnists and celebrities collaborated in an unspoken ritual of career enhancement and the Copa was the beneficiary. And thanks to Jimmy Durante I also made the columns in those early days, reportedly being seen with eligible or well-known celebrities.

Not everyone who came to the Copa wanted dinner and a floorshow. Some just wanted a congenial watering hole where they could meet friends and see and be seen. The Lounge was that kind of place. It could accommodate 30 patrons seated on velvet-covered bar stools. The same velvet covered the banquettes along the other wall, with small tables occupying the center of the room. It was glamorous, but informal, and was filled to overflowing every night. Jack Eigen broadcasted a live radio show from the Lounge nightly on station WMGM (he was succeeded by one of the eventual giants of talk radio, Barry Gray). All sorts of celebrities from the world of politics, sports, and of course show business—sometimes even the stars actually working at the Copa that night—would show up to be interviewed. Jack's program began at 10 p.m. and ran until 4 a.m. in the morning. Many people would stay there all evening listening to Jack's guests and staring (discretely) at the celebrities and big shots that were in the Lounge. On a good night, you could see a "Who's Who" in that room.

Celebrities liked the Lounge not only for the chance to be interviewed, but also for its discreet ambiance. They were allowed to be themselves without people pestering them for autographs and the like. The club staff was very efficient in its efforts to make favored customers and famous visitors feel comfortable. If a private party was required, the Lounge had a small, but cozy, secret room where privileged guests could slip in inconspicuously and meet (a custom that many famous clubs, like Studio 54, later copied). I always thought that a lot of really big deals were consummated in that room, a part of the Copa's legend.

To get from the Lounge to the Copa's main show room you went down a staircase from the lobby and you were in what was called "the big room." The dance floor itself was sunken, surrounded by tables and artificial palm trees (lots of palm trees!) arranged in tiers. Tables were placed in the semicircle facing the dance floor. There were also a few tables on the floor itself, ringside—the best seats in the house. A small stage area was flanked by two sets of staircases, about three steps each, the ones I descended on my maiden appearance. The small bandstand was off to one side.

The decor was tropical. White palm trees were placed next to mirrors painted with green palm fronds, interspersed between beautiful red and white draperies; heavily enhanced by white fringes. To complete the Brazilian effect, and maybe to match our incredible hats, the drapes were adorned with Carmen Miranda imitation fruit. The lighting was influenced Art Deco, projecting soft blue and pink hues. The VIP seating—the banquettes against the wall, a preferred place for columnists and others who liked to see, rather than be seen—sported red velvet.

The size of the crowd in the main room was of some concern to the dancers, because on a busy night they'd add tables wherever they could leaving less space and turning our routine into more of an obstacle course. The seating—referred to as "flexible"—could balloon from 670 to 1500. And it wasn't just the dancers that were affected; the additional tables squeezed the customers and the orchestra as well. Sometimes, when it was a really packed, we'd be prancing around and dodging some guy's feet, or on infrequent occasions, usually at the last show, you'd have to be alert or you'd get pinched or grabbed by some guy who had too much to drink. Of course they learned how rapidly the Copa could give the heave-ho to an overexcited ringsider. The club didn't permit that kind of stuff. But, because liquor was part of the entertainment and some of our customers were sometimes a long way from home, things did happen.

The first time I saw professional dancers I was a teenager. I gazed in wonder at the huge domed ceiling and broad, tall stage of New York's Radio City Music Hall. The Rockettes were amazing and I clapped as hard as I could at their precision and their complicated routines. They were so far away that I couldn't see their faces, to see if they were smiling and enjoying their work as thousands of people applauded. The difference between that stage and this tiny little Copa stage was dramatic, but everyone in the Copa audience could see my face; I was grinning ear to ear.

Compared to other nightspots in the city, the Copa was the elite, and represented 1940's popular culture in miniature. It attracted more of the famous and the well-heeled than any other night spot; show biz people, sports figures, especially jockeys and prize fighters, business magnates from Seventh Avenue or Wall Street, Texas oilmen, wealthy businessmen from South America, bookmakers, producers, high-ranking mobsters (like Albert Anastasia and Frank

Costello), war profiteers, war heroes (a temporary celebrity status), Hollywood celebrities, and anyone who had a reputation as a big tipper.

Everybody needed a reservation—unless you were among the superstars, or a close friend of the maitre d's, Joe Lopez, Gus or Arthur Brown. They were the official greeters at the club, and the enforcers as well. Their word was law. They knew who was famous and who was a pretender; they knew all the families in Society's blue book, the Mafia, the politicians, and of course the columnists. They also knew who was on the Copa's black list, who the girls in the line were dating, and which headliners needed what food or drink in their dressing rooms. Columnists crossed their palms with money and some "mentions," if they were treated right. And unless a columnist stepped out of line and printed something that somebody important didn't like, they were granted every courtesy.

With three opulent shows a night, and a famous headliner, in those days, a seat—any seat—at the Copa, was a treasure, and many a high roller who wanted a ringside table became instant friends with Joe Lopez, the most famous of those at the rope, with the transfer of a rolled-up $100 bill. Joe never forgot a face or the size of a tip. Some reports had each of the three rope-guardians averaging $1000 a night.

The Copa was not a tourist stop, unless you were a well-heeled and well-known tourist, such as royalty from Europe or a movie star vacationing in the city. It had virtually no convention goers (conventions didn't become common until after the war, and even then, the Copa was not on their bus routes), weekend or summer tourists who came to New York City in later years. Those types went to the clubs such as the Latin Quarter, the Martinique, or Billy Rose' Diamond Horseshoe on Broadway, or any of the other places that counted on the tourist trade.

In keeping with the ambiance of glamorous exclusivity, women came to the Copa dressed in evening gowns, hats, furs, lovely jewelry, white ermine and sable wraps—all except for Miss Dietrich, who fashioned the Tuxedo look for women. Men too wore evening tuxedos or dinner jackets with satin lapels. Courtship was a ritual at ringside. Rich men from all over the world sent white orchids to the girls backstage; often containing little treasures, like a diamond bracelet, expensive rings and pearls in velvet boxes with love notes. And, of course Champagne was always popular (though Jules Podell would not allow us to open it until the end of the night).

If someone had a table for the 8 p.m. dinner show, they'd get a terrific meal expertly cooked and elegantly served, with a choice of good wines or fine mixed drinks. Chinese dishes were the specialty, but there were other cuisines as well. There was a $3 minimum in effect, but never a cover charge. Meals ranged in price from $4.95 for a ham omelet to $6.40 for a Chicken-a-la-King on toast, up to $7.95 for tenderloin of prime beef Stroganoff. A jumbo shrimp cocktail was $3.35. Coffee was 80 cents, beer 90 cents, a Martini and most other mixed drinks cost $1.70, except for a Bloody Mary ($2) or a mint julep ($2.40). The average working guy back then earned $40.00 a week! Of course, the average guy didn't go to the Copa. Its lifeblood was from repeat customers. The regulars weren't just regular at the Copa; they were frequent. If the price and the food weren't right, the Copa's generally affluent, sophisticated nightlife crowd wouldn't be there. Of course the main reason you came to the Copa was to see and hear the star—the headliner. The Copa carved out a distinct niche for itself with the talent it presented. For the most part, the headliners were on the brink of being major stars, or were major stars already. The saying went "that if you had a successful run at the Copa, you were almost guaranteed stardom." Many of those stars made return trips to the Copa, even after they no longer did nightclub gigs, to see what the up-and-coming talent was like, and as recognition to where they had their first huge success.

So, needless to say that when I started my own fully-fledged show career there I was in good—in fact great—company.

CHAPTER 7

Stately Showgirls and Dainty Ponies

Swimming in the Aquacade had pushed me into the swift morning waters of show business, but it was the Copa that got me into the deep end. The day after our opening, it was a Broadway columnist who reminded me of how far I had come. At 7:00 a.m. I got a call from my sister, who shouted at me excitedly: "Harriet, your name's in the paper! Her mood was infectious. I had to rush out and buy a paper. Lo and behold, in the New York Mirror, in the most famous of all the Broadway columns, Walter Winchell wrote: "Monte Proser's Copacabana opened last night and is the latest click on East 60th St. Jimmy Durante and Harriet Weber, a front line pony (show biz for a not-tall dancer), partying after the show…"

I probably needed Winchell to remind me of where I'd been the night before; one of seven girls in the Copacabana chorus line, having dinner afterwards at Reubens with Jimmy Durante and all those people whose names I couldn't remember now, but would see again later on. This was the nightclub set, those people who loved the glitter and glamour of Manhattan's nightlife. They liked to be in beautiful places and around famous people (of course many of them were famous people). During the day some might be idle playboys, important executives knocking down big money, stars, or even struggling wannabe entertainers looking for the right connection. But at night, with a ringside table at the Copa, they were the lords of Broadway. They were noticed by everybody present and if later in the evening were seen in an after hours joint with a Copa girl, their stock rose mightily. If they were lucky, a Broadway columnist—ever alert for a hot item—might even inquire as to who they were.

If I had been a chorus line dancer on opening night at any other place, despite being seen with Jimmy Durante afterwards, I doubt whether I'd have gotten mentioned. But that's the effect the Copa had on columnists from the very beginning. They seemed to know the Copa and its people were very special. Over the next few years I was spotted with many well-known people at various hot spots around town, and that alone was enough to fuel columnists into quick speculation. I never knew any of this when I first became a Copa pony. I had no idea that this sort of world existed, but I took to it immediately. I had a thrilling social life. And though many of the mentions were pure conjecture, the papers printed it anyway.

I had only been dating John a short time, when Dorothy Kilgallen (Journal American) picked up on it and wrote: "Is the President's son John Roosevelt eyeing Harriet Weber and sending orchids backstage at the Copacabana?" Actually, yes he was. And dating the president's son was like living in a fairytale. He was tall and good-looking and I accompanied him to many parties and functions. I quickly noticed though that wherever we were, he never had any cash with him. He explained that he didn't need it. He could just sign for everything, wherever he was (he never shopped in convenience stores, after all), and at the end of the month the accountant would pay for everything. I realized that the life of the rich and famous was indeed different from the masses, but the John Roosevelt's of the world were in a league all their own. I'm sure that he probably thought that carrying cash, as most people do, was odd.

After the last show at the Copa one night, John was called over by Peggy Lee, and I asked him afterwards, "What's it like to be famous"? He gave me a smile and said, "I'm not famous, Peanuts (his nickname for me), my father's famous, I'm just his son." John was like that: down to Earth and easy going despite the

Harry Ritz & Harriet

privileged life he was living. Our relationship evolved into a friendship, and it would be decades before I saw him again, but we remained friends until his death.

I had many dinner dates and they seemed to all make the columns. Louis Sobel, in his "New York Cavalcade" column, noted "Copacabana Veteran Press Agent Ted Howard reported seeing Copacabeaut, the lovely Harriet Weber at Reuben's restaurant with Sam Bramson for the Wm. Morris Agency..." Ed Sullivan posed a question in his Little Old New York column, "Is Harry Ritz of the famous Ritz Brothers carrying on a 4-alarm blaze with Harriet Weber—Copacabana cutie?" No Ed, he wasn't. But everyone seemed to love the Copa girls, and of course, I loved that they loved us.

It wasn't all dinner dates and gossip columns however. I worked hard, not only at dancing, but also at the Copa "look." This meant Brazilian accents and an upswept hairdo. Since costumes changed with every new production, the hair could be changed—drastically—as often as every three months and dyed to coordinate with the color of the costume. As a result, a Copa pony (or one of the Samba Sirens, as we were also known) would, over time, have hair that was colored red, pink, green, orange, or purple; whatever was needed to blend with the outfit—even though most times our hair was covered with the famous Copa headdress. Sometimes, I thought that all those changing vivid hair colors must have really confused some of the regular customers who often had one drink too many.

Paradoxically, our tropical glamour was applied to its opposite: the typical Copa girl was a blonde haired, blue-eyed, fair-skinned young woman who looked like the ideal girl-next-door. Maybe it was this peaches-and-cream look that prompted Walter Winchell to report that the "paying customers who came back with endearing regularity were impressed by the Copacabana girls. It's the best girl show in town." In other words, we were sultry, but safe. It was the same look that captured the attention of Hollywood. By 1943 Life Magazine reported that Hollywood recognized that the Copa was a gold mine for young talent. We looked like small-town unspoiled women too young to be out after dark. In some cases, appearances were certainly deceiving!

The Copa wasn't the only nitery to strive for its own special look, but it was the only one that carried the idea to such exacting, uniform standards. When we went through our five routines, simple though they were, everyone's eyes were upon us—the customers, the staff—especially management. We were as practiced and skilled a set of dancers as were to be found in any Broadway show. If we weren't good enough there were hundreds of other girls eager to take our places; casting calls for new dancers went out about every three months, and hundreds showed up each time. So, we took our job seriously.

Club policy only permitted each girl to be hired for one three-month engagement at a time—the clientele demanded a lot of variety in its choice of blondes in the 1940s. Despite all the girls at our heels that wanted our jobs, we were also driven by pride and knew that a spectacular performance could be a stepping-stone for other career opportunities, especially Hollywood! Some Copa girls in later years got there, including June Allyson, Joanne Dru, May Wynn, Janice Rule, and Lucille Bremer, to name just a few. The possibility of Hollywood was something I dreamed of too. Anyone who was ever told she was beautiful and talented hoped for a shot at the movies.

The money for those days was good—$75 a week, which certainly wasn't "star" money, but was more than some of the blue color jobs I mentioned earlier ($40 a week). It was quite a contrast to the estimates that each Copa costume cost an average of $1500; bedecked with sequins, mink (bras, matching muffs, panties, hats), or any one of many other themes and styles. Bottom line, they were lavish and expensive.

Doing shows every night always presented the possibility for unexpected folly: you just never knew what could happen from night to night. There we were bouncing along in a routine that required a high kick. Without warning one of the girl's high-heeled shoes sailed into the audience, into the lap of actor/comedian Phil Silvers. Sitting ringside—then at the top of his career—he leaped up as if he had been given an electric shock. We, of course, kept on dancing as if nothing had happened (although the girl who lost the shoe had a definite up-and-down motion to her dancing). Silvers made a big to-do about returning the shoe limping, of course, to milk every laugh from the incident. The audience whistled, applauded and laughed, while the offending chorus girl blushed bright red. Later, not knowing if Don Loper would be angry, or if the girl was in danger of being fired, we lightheartedly suggested that we ought to keep that lost-shoe business in the act. Don looked mock serious and said, "Only if we can guarantee Phil Silvers will be there to catch it every night."

I was in the audience years later during a show in 1948, headlined by Jerry Lewis and Dean Martin, when the hook-and-eye clasp on Evelynn Peterson's (now Olrich) skirt broke, causing her zipper to open. While she danced on unaware and intent on avoiding further collisions, she kept hearing people say 'Psst!' Finally, realizing what was happening, she held her Carmen Miranda hat with one hand and grabbed her skirt clutched around her waist with the other, while Jack Entratter glared at her from back stage. Her night improved when Ethel Merman (a Broadway star) came backstage to chat and admire her makeup, and then Mel Torme asked her for a date, which she accepted. Copa girls didn't always receive offers from stars. Lynne Galvin (a model for many national brands) was a Copa girl in the '50s when a fan offered to marry her so they could live together and raise chickens on Long Island (needless to say she turned him down).

Evelynn Peterson

One of the most popular women at the Copa during my time there wasn't even in the show. Anya was a blonde beauty gorgeous enough to be in the line, who had in fact been a dancer years earlier with her partner Diego. But in the 1940's she was a palmist, averaging 40 readings an evening (earning hundreds of dollars) peering by match light at a customer's palm and conveying the good or bad news. With her hair pulled up in swirling spirals over a black velvet frame to create a glamorous and aloof look, she had more style than skill. Still, the customers loved it, as did LIFE Magazine, who wrote about her in an article they did about the Copa.

Most of the girls cherished their Copa days as magical, not only for the on-stage experiences, but also for the off stage life that being a Copa girl provided. Fay Suter, Miss Fort Wayne 1948, was another protégé of Jimmy Durante. She dated Johnny Carson, was good friends with Frank Sinatra, Ava Gardner, and Joe DiMaggio, and was married briefly to actor Ted Jordan (of TV's Gunsmoke). By 1956 she went on to Broadway in the musical Lil'l Abner and enjoyed a successful modeling and acting career. She appeared in 133 TV commercials before becoming a senior vice-president of Promenade Magazine. We kept in touch until she died in 1995, at age 64.

Our "workdays" were upside down: we worked all night, partied until dawn, and slept afternoons until it was time to go to work again. It was exhausting, but rarely dull. The company we kept was the envy of many. The perks, like backstage trinkets from stage-door johnnies, were a nice touch too. It told us we were something special, and we believed it. But, Fran Paige Schenkel also recalls that to keep them (the stage-door Johnnies) from getting "too thrilled," there were matrons that sheltered the girls from prying visitors and kept their noses clean. She liked that, as well as the policy of not allowing the dancers to sit out front unescorted when they weren't dancing, or allowing them to mingle with the guests. "It was designed to keep our mind on our work and protect our reputations as well as the club's," she said. Only under certain circumstances, and with the permission of Jules Podell could a dancer sit in the audience. Fran was one of the few permitted to do so, at the special request of high profile Copa customer Howard Huges—the normally reclusive millionaire—who invited Fran to sit at his banquette often when he was in town.

Many of the practicing Catholic girls in the line would go to the Actor's Chapel (which still exists today on Theater Row in New York) mass after the last show on Saturday. Many times drunks and other pests bothered them as they walked to the church in the wee hours of the morning. Danny Thomas heard about the trouble the girls were having (during one of his Copa appearances) and, as a Catholic himself, sympathized because he often had to attend mass at odd hours. So, he visited the local police precinct, talked to the church staff and, most important, told Walter Winchell that those nice Copa girls were being annoyed as they went to church on their way home from work. Winchell reported this on his radio program and, as if by magic, the girls were not bothered anymore. It was this respect for the Copa girl that Fran remembers most—that and the fact that being a Copa girl enabled her to meet the man in her life, TV sports announcer Chris Schenkel.

Meanwhile, I was about to begin another three-month Copa tour.

CHAPTER 8

End Of An Era

Our first show started at eight (the dinner show), and the next began at midnight. If we didn't have a dinner date after the last show, sometimes we'd go on short dates between shows. More often than not when we did the "scramble" between shows we'd have our dates waiting for us at the restaurant. There was never much time to linger, but it was a way to get a good meal. Needless to say, Jules Podell frowned on this practice. In fact, he forbade it. He said it was OK to run out for an errand—a quick bite to eat or to pick up take out—but not in our costumes and no dates! Girls had been fired for violating his rules, but we were young and brash, so we did it anyway. There were four of us ready to do the eight to midnight "scramble" for a date with four guys. With our winter coats over our Copa costumes and little suitcases in hand, we hailed a cab and gave him an uptown address. "Hurry," we said. We were hungry.

He gunned the motor and headed uptown while the four of us began to change clothes. It was a tight fit in that backseat, even though it was one of those roomy old Checker cabs. We yanked, pulled and elbowed one another, all the while trying to control our laughter: it was a comic scene. Our efforts drew the driver's attention and as best he could without smashing into something, he kept looking in the rearview mirror. We arrived at the restaurant, paid off the driver, and scurried inside to have dinner. Afterwards, we grabbed another cab and hurried back downtown, changing on the fly as before.

As we neared the Copa, Jules Podell was waiting for us, fuming. He said someone saw us having dinner, and he reminded us—quite forcefully—that we weren't supposed to leave the club for dates. One of us asked him how he knew we were out to dinner, and he said that someone told him. We pressed him: "Who told you? How did they know we were Copa girls?" Finally, to impress upon us that we couldn't put one over on him, he told us the cabdriver told him personally. We were furious. "That lecherous so-and-so," we said, and were so steamed that we were ready to rebel. But we didn't want to antagonize Jules any further—he was the boss after all and let us off with a warning. That was a close call, although it never stopped us from doing it again.

Money was never a concern when we went out since there were always people around eager to buy a hungry Copa girl a meal and a drink. As with our looks (the girl next door Blonde), there were also established beliefs about our dining habits. "Take a Copa girl to dinner," went the current saying and, "she'll always order a shrimp cocktail and a big steak." Dating was fun of course, but sometimes our basic needs came first. When the last show was over at about 4 a.m. and we were through removing makeup, and hanging up clothes, we'd usually be famished. Only rarely did we ever get to eat the Copa food. For some reason the kitchen was Podell's special little empire, though it never made much money. Still, he spent a lot of time there yelling at the cooks. It would have been awkward to get food at the Copa, and against club policy to eat it even if we did. So when the last show was over, we just wanted out of that place.

More often than not, when there wasn't a hot date to impress or be impressed by, our first stop after work was Reubens. It was big, noisy, and invigorating. This is where we disproved that saying about "our eating habits"—breakfast food was the staple fare here, not shrimp cocktails. The specialty of the house was apple pancakes—as well as impromptu and outrageous floorshows by whatever comedians happen to be dinning there at the moment: they were always "on."

If we were going out for a few drinks, on the spur of the moment after the show, we liked the company of bartenders. They were good sports, good tippers, and they always looked out for us. We felt safe with them. (In those days bartending was a profession, not just something out-of-work actors or college students did.) The times were different back then, and people didn't fall into bed with one another casually as they seem to do today. A guy looking for a date meant he'd like to escort the girl to a late supper, or a few drinks, or catch the last floorshow at some other club. Time didn't matter because there were after hour places all over the area, the most famous being the exclusive Gold Key Club on West 56th Street near 7th Avenue, owned by Vinny Bruno. Anyone who wanted to continue drinking or had a special girlfriend to impress took their dates there—if they could get in. It was members only. This was literally one of those places where you rang the bell and waited to be "recognized" before the buzzer let you in—another remnant of the old speakeasy tradition.

Set inside a brownstone building, like its neighbors, it had heavy glass panels on the front door. The doormen always let Copa girls in, as well as girls from other clubs, because after all the prospect of meeting beautiful chorus girls was what drew the men there. But it wasn't a pick up joint. Vinny made sure the girls weren't pestered. Once in the foyer, you followed a curved dark-oak staircase to the second floor. The whole effect was low-key, upscale elegance. Inside the softly lit dining area you'd probably see some of the people you just left at the Copa, as well as people from other clubs you came to know. It had expensive comfortable furniture and a well stocked bar and kitchen. As a member you could run a tab. Specialty of the house was southern-style biscuits, chicken and gravy and it was scrumptious.

We'd come in at 4:00 a.m., maybe later, either with a date or in a bunch (we girls often had more fun being with each other than some strange guy you might or might not end up liking). It was very civilized and an ideal place to relax after a hard night.

Being a Copa girl often provided a back door pass to the most elite of the social scene too. When Frank Sinatra was in town he held open house at his suite at the Waldorf Astoria, for instance. A good host, he liked to pour drinks and order food over the phone. Fun was as abundant at a Sinatra party as liquor was. I found him to be quite charming. Like good Champaign, having a Copa girl or two on hand was de rigueur for a smart party. We were there to dress up the event; smile, laugh, and listen to stories. We didn't mind. We were used to backing up the stars. I had to pinch myself sometimes just to realize that I was really there. Frank's parties were fabulous, but there was a catch; you couldn't leave until Frank said so—if you wanted to be invited back for the next one. It was his party and he was the Chairman of the Board.

When Danny Stradella (owner of Danny's Hideaway) would come into the club in the 1950s, he would often invite the entire chorus line back to his club after hours for celebrity parties. There, girls might see anybody from John F. Kennedy to Elvis Presley. Jewel Peterson was among them. She went on to perform with the Rat Pack at the Sands Hotel in Las Vegas, where she received a surprise birthday cake from Frank/Dino/Sammy, and then later appeared with them in the film Oceans Eleven (the original version). But it was at the Copa where she first started her entertainment career and met many celebrities that she would go on to enjoy long friendships with.

Jewel was a Copa girl for three tours (nine months) and managed to get herself fired everyday! She liked to stroll through the kitchen to say hello to the staff, and for some reason that drove Podell nuts. So he'd fire her on the spot (with the much banging of his famous ring). It never seemed to faze her though, and before the end of the night choreographer Doug Coudy would always tell her she was being given "another chance." Eventually she married Steve Bregman, an executive with Caesar's Hotels in Las Vegas.

By the 1960's Susan Seton's AGVA (American Guild of Variety Artists) contract stipulated a salary of $150 a week (which was exactly double what I was paid when I joined the line in 1940). Columnists in those days were still making big deals about much-a-do about nothing, as a way of getting the names of pretty show business people, especially those at the Copa, before the public. Walter Winchell (and other Broadway writers) noted that Susan, having just turned 18 years old, had to bring a birth certificate to prove her age, as though that was really newsworthy information. It would appear that she did dance at the Copa a short while before she attained the legal age.

I think back to when I was a teenager, even younger than Susan, when I was still in high school and my friends and I would be so star-struck that we would cut school to attend concerts at the Paramount Theater. Frank Sinatra was there on one such occasion and we danced uncontrollably in the aisles, screaming as though we would just die if he stopped singing. Funny, I started out dancing in front of the stars, and ended up dancing behind them. Having all that talent out in front of us as Copa girls made for anything but routine workdays. But, sometimes, the headliner couldn't resist the crowd's urging for "more, more, more!" This was good for the audience, but not so good for us. One such performer was the then famous comedian Joe E. Lewis, who had a gravelly voice, compliments of a Mafia thug who cut his throat over some dispute. This didn't slow Joe down at all. He liked to continue until he dropped.

He'd be fully clothed when he first came out, but as his act progressed he'd get drunk and start removing his clothes. When he got down to his shorts people would begin to hold their breath, but he never went further. His favorite thing was to shout "It's Post Time!" and then grab a customer's drink and down it. He'd do that several times during his act, but no one ever complained. In fact, it was an "honor" to have him polish off your drink. He was one of the first—and best—"insult" sort of comedians, and audiences loved him.

Sometimes it took Lewis an hour or more after his scheduled finish to finally end his act. In the meantime we would be there in the background standing in our famous Copa pose, arms interlocked, waiting for the final cue to close the show. We saw a lot more of Joe E. Lewis than we wanted to, but he won our hearts nonetheless. Luckily for us, if actor Don Ameche or Ben Marden (who ran the Rivera; the best after-hours and gambling club in New Jersey) were in the audience, he gave each Copa girl a $100 tip for the extra effort.

The Copa featured every popular act in show business at one time or another, but one of my favorites was Nat King Cole. He wasn't a good-looking man, but he was a true gentleman, not to mention a great showman that brought in huge crowds. Once inside the club, like the other performers, he got a free room upstairs in the Hotel 14, above the Copa quarters. But, this was the 1940's, long before civil rights, and even though he was one of show business' most professional, best-loved singers, he still couldn't use the front door to enter the Club. Like most of the other "hired help" he had to use the service entrance, and always make his way to the stage via the kitchen. Despite this ungracious treatment he received, he was always graciousness himself. After every show he would give all the help gold cufflinks with the Copa logo, and gold earrings to the dancers.

When my neighbors saw me in my Copa outfits I might draw some oohs and ahhs. Perhaps I seemed like some kind of celebrity to them when we met in the hallways. But in the club I was part of the scenery; just like the palm trees and South American atmosphere, all there to back up the star attraction. Still, it was fun—after all, we were the most famous scenery in New York City. We stayed with our kind, entertainers, because not many other working people had the routines we did. And, unless we had steady boyfriends, we spent many of our off-hours together. In addition to breakfast at Reubens, or an after-hours club, we would do other things together, such as go to Ebbets Field for the ladies day matinee and cheer for the Brooklyn Dodgers (long before they moved to Los Angeles). We'd go roller-skating or ice-skating, or anything that seemed like it would be fun.

Years later, I wasn't working at the club when Dean Martin and Jerry Lewis began appearing in the 1950's, before their movie successes, but I was often in the audience. To me, they weren't as enjoyable as Joe E. Lewis or the singers such as Tony Bennett, Frank Sinatra, Eddie Fisher or Vic Damone, but the crowd sure seemed to enjoy them. Some of the female stars included Jane Powell, Patti Page, Connie Francis, and Lena Horne—who finally forced the Club to stop its segregated entrance policy. Of special interest to those of us in the line was Olga San Juan, who progressed from Copa girl to featured night-club singer to Broadway star: she played the leading lady in the 1940's Lerner & Lowe hit musical *Paint Your Wagon*. I'm happy to say I saw them all, either from the stage as a Copa girl or from the audience in later years.

I wasn't the only performer who enjoyed being in the audience. Show business types working in other clubs—from chorus line dancers to headliners—would often come to catch the last show—the one where the best crowds were on hand and all the unpredictable things happened. Baseball great Mickey Mantle is still associated with the Copa by old-timers who remember an argument that began in the club and escalated into a brawl on the sidewalk out front, involving him and other legendary New York Yankee baseball stars: Billy Martin, Hank Bauer, Whitey Ford, and Roger Maris. Naturally the newspapers picked up on the story. Instead of getting negative publicity the Copa became even more popular (if that were possible).

By the 1960s New York City had begun imposing a new cabaret tax on nightclubs, even though the city was in a temporary tourist slump. The social changes, as well as changes in legislation and tax laws, meant the slow disintegration of the clubs and the lifestyle they represented. In 1969 the Copa and Jules Podell both died the same year, and with their passing came the end of an era.

CHAPTER 9

Go West Young Girl, Go West

It seems to be a fact of life that if you work in and around the entertainment business, sooner or later you run into the mob. I'll leave it to others to explain why that's so, but it is. At the height of the nightclub era they had an interest in a number of the clubs, including, of course, the Copa, though their presence didn't affect our day-to-day routine. Most of the "wise" guys we met seemed just like regular guys, doing whatever they did without talking about it—and like other guys, they liked to be around pretty girls. Usually they had lots of spending money, so the girls liked to be around them too. But I don't want you to get the impression that life was like some scene from the musical *42nd Street*—slick juveniles and gold diggers. Though there certainly were a few, it wasn't the majority.

Except for a few pieces of jewelry and some things to wear, I didn't "collect" things from admirers the way some of the girls did. Their Copa status was worth far more to them than what they were paid in salary. Ever since show biz was show biz, there have been men drawn to chorus girls like bees to honey; maybe it's the old myth about chorus girls being promiscuous or easy to manipulate or whatever. Or maybe it's simply because most young girls in show business are beautiful, and what man isn't drawn to a pretty girl? There were young women who took advantage of those things: in some cases presents weren't the only thing these girls wanted. Some of them sought out and found husbands, rich husbands. Others made connections in the movies or other parts of show business; some merely settled down with some ordinary-type guy they happened to love, content to marry the boy-next-door type and raise a family. Either way, the Copa, in almost every case, was a stepping stone to somewhere else.

I began another tour as a Copa Girl, committed to another three months of coming down those steps to all that applause and looking ahead to another zany night of laughs and champagne, steak and quick dates between shows. Also, meeting all those famous people and getting love notes from stage door Johnnies and "thank you" gifts of all kinds for having dinner with a rich guy. Would you believe one guy gave me a 27-carat aquamarine ring with rubies—which had to cost $4000 at that time—just because I went to dinner with him? Somehow though, as exciting and glamorous as all this seemed, I was getting tired of the routine. Yes, there were lots of benefits and I never lacked for excitement, glamour, clothing or good meals, but I wasn't going anywhere. I'd seen lots of girls leave the Copa line go to California to make movies, or marry young and rich businessmen and move to Darien Connecticut, never having to work again. My salary alone certainly didn't provide security—I wasn't saving any money on $75 a week.

There was also another recent source of irritation in my life, Ben. After my mother died, he sold the house in Brooklyn and secretly remarried. His new wife, Bea, who we thought was a girlfriend, was a constant nagging presence. She didn't like the fact that my sister Terri and I were living with him; didn't approve of our jobs, and generally made life miserable for us. She was a bitch and he was becoming nasty just like her. Here he was, someone who chased every skirt in Brooklyn when he was married to my mother and making his fortune, lecturing me about taking a few bucks from a guy who had plenty and only wanted a pretty dinner companion. Talk about your double standards. Even as a young girl I never related much to Ben, but now with the knowledge that he wasn't really my real father the connection was even less. So when he started to ride me for taking tip money from "strange" men, it began to fester under my skin.

I knew what he was insinuating. Sure there were guys on the make, looking for a sexual adventure with a beautiful chorine, but they didn't find it with me, nor any of the Copa girls I knew and went on double dates with. Sometimes a date did evolve into a romance and even marriage. Some Copa girls did go onto marry rich industrialists, entertainment people or wealthy sons of aging millionaires, but even the ones that didn't weren't available to guys on the make. My own involvement with men of extraordinary wealth was limited to only two. I had told you about John Roosevelt, who evolved into more of a friend than a romance, and then there was John Jacob Astor III. A bunch of us often met up with him (JJ as I called him) at his penthouse after a show, where he had the whole floor. We began to date and I even escorted him to parties at the family mansion.

The family home is exactly what you would expect from an old money family: traditional and grand. It was the most beautiful New York City home I had ever seen, with over 15 rooms and electronic alarm systems everywhere to protect all the artwork and expensive furnishings. The family, though a little on the stuffy side, were perfectly polite. I guess they were used to their playboy children bringing home entertainers. I was still a little too young to appreciate much of what it was then, but I knew it was out of my league socially.

Why, you might ask, didn't I play it smart and become his steady girl friend, or maybe even his wife? Simple, JJ liked his liquor too much and I have always been uncomfortable around heavy drinkers; I never met a drunk I liked! I would meet a lot of people at these after-hours parties, rich and famous ones especially, and some of the girls latched onto them as quickly as they could, regardless of the habits or personality of these men. Not me, there had to be something more than money to get my attention. Also, JJ wasn't really dependable. I found out later, according to another Copa girl he courted, that he actually proposed and took her on a cruise to Europe as a pre-wedding trip. En route, he happened to see her passport and noticed her birth date. Whatever it was, she was too old, in JJ's estimation, so he dropped her. But the rich playboys were like that; they could have what, or whomever they wanted, whenever they wanted, so they got bored easily. I guess, my instinct about him was correct.

This was the madcap show business culture in which I was living, and it was one that Ben didn't understand, so a flare up was inevitable. I came home as usual about seven in the morning, and I was telling Terri about my "work day." Ben Marden had given me (and the other dancers) a tip after another unusually long Joe E. Lewis finale. It was a great show and the crowd had howled and drunk their expensive liquor while we seven girls stood, waiting for the end. It happened before—it would happen again—that's show biz at the Copa. But we were given $100 each as a thank you.

Ben came into the kitchen just in time to hear the tail end of the conversation. He hadn't heard the first part of the story, nor did he inquire. He put on a righteous attitude and started calling me names. He demanded that I promise I'd give the money back, or give it to him and he'd take it back. I said no, and he called me a tramp. "How dare you," I protested. He continued his tirade and then I cut him off, "Enough! I'm moving out!" Terri, who was 16 at the time, said she was coming too, because some of that tirade was aimed at her, since she was performing in a production of Peter Pan in Manhattan and her hours were as crazy as mine. Ben was stunned and just stood there. Bea was delighted (now she could move in and be an official wife.)

At first we moved in with some Copa girls I knew and shared a grand apartment. But shortly after they both got engaged, so Terri and I took a room at the Belmont Plaza Hotel, across from the Waldorf Astoria Hotel on Lexington Avenue. It was a bit pricey for us, but we were determined to find a way to stay on our own. I was still in the middle of my tour at the Copa, and that would provide us a little cash until something else turned up. Something did turn up, and quite inadvertently; Ben was the cause of it. We had been living there for about a month when Ben called and asked us to join him for dinner at the hotel—it would be his treat. Reluctantly we agreed, knowing he'd be pleading for us to return. We figured his apartment must be a very gloomy place without Terri's laughter and my busy comings and going.

So we went to dinner, and, as expected, Ben asked us to return. His wife would change, he said—"Oh sure…," I thought—and he wouldn't criticize us any more, he said. I listened politely then said "no." Terri nodded in agreement. Ben tried and tried, but we were adamant. We liked living here, we said. The argument went back and forth. At the next table, unnoticed by me, sat three men—Jesse Lasky, Jr., Richard Brooks, and David Lord. I didn't register Lord's constant glances because I was so busy dealing with Ben. (I learned later that once David Lord noticed me he couldn't take his eyes off me.)

David was listening when I mentioned which room I lived in, and when Terri and I got home from our shows later that night, David was sitting on the floor next to the door. "Don't I know you from somewhere?" he asked with a smile. I responded in a friendly manner, and picked up his cue. "Oh, yes, it must have been in Atlantic City." He laughed and we laughed. He was staying in the same hotel, which he said was an omen. He had a very winning manner and easy style, and he quickly made us feel we had nothing to fear. He began to tell me that he was a writer and about his important friends. I'd heard a lot of this stuff before, from better bull-throwers than he, but he was charming and funny. His published novels included Joey and The Ravenger, and he was connected to Hollywood because one of his books was sold for a movie. I didn't know how those things happened, but I was led to believe that David was a fairly big man in Hollywood.

He knew people there, he said. His parents lived there. The world he described was tantalizing. Maybe someday, I thought, I too would find a place in Hollywood. After all, I knew the stories. Other chorus girls were discovered in New York and flown first-class to Hollywood to become rich and famous. Why not me? So there, in the corridor of the hotel, David and I had our first date. I had no idea of the series of events that were about to follow.

David would come to see me at the Copa regularly. Columnist Danton Walker wrote in the Gotham Gazette—"…the Story Tellers of Hollywood:

Screen Writers Jesse Lasky Jr., Richard Brooks and David Lord, in town to make studio war training films, sitting ringside at the Copacabana. Was the stage attraction pretty dancer Harriet Weber the reason David Lord is planning on seeing a preacher?"

Fate sometimes seems to have a way of moving everything in the same direction. David and I had only been dating a few weeks when I received a call one night. I answered and heard a familiar, hoarse voice using my pet name "Henrietta, is that you Henrietta? This is Jimmy Durate, your long lost uncle." I screamed with such delight that Terri thought I was frightened. "Henrietta, pack your bag," he continued. "You've been at the Copa long enough. So now it's time to move on. I got just the place for you." I held by breath. "You mean Hollywood?" I asked, hoping madly but expecting to be told something else. "Right, Henrietta, my darling Aquacade lovely. My good friend Esther Williams is going to make her first movie, she's a terrific swimmer, and she needs some good swimmers to keep her company when the camera rolls."

I was stunned! The movies! And swimming? Whoever this Esther Williams was, she couldn't be any harder to work for than Billy Rose. I didn't hesitate. My Copa contract was coming to an end and I was ready for something new. "Where do I go when I get there, and what time do we start?" While he talked, my thoughts were racing: "I don't have any money and I've never been to California. Wait. I can live with Needy (my sister who had been living in Los Angeles now for a several years). I can do it!" I nearly cheered out loud—almost not hearing Jimmy's instructions. "Don't take too long to get here," he said. "They'll be casting pretty soon, maybe any day now, so move fast, and call me when you arrive and I'll set things up. OK, Henrietta? I gotta go."

He was gone, and I was holding the dead telephone receiver realizing how much my life changed in a minute or so. I also had a few problems, the biggest being how to get a train ticket to California without a cent to my name. I didn't want to ask Ben, I had to find my own way. Then I began to worry about Terri. At 16, could she live alone? Should I take her with me? Would she want to come? Or would she go back to Ben's place? My mind wandered back to David. He was attractive and funny, and after only a few short weeks wanted to marry me. And he was going back to California. I liked him but had been resisting his advances. Although I enjoyed sex as much as anybody, I guess, I knew then (at 22 years old) that when something goes wrong with a love affair, it's usually the woman who gets hurt, unless she has some insurance—like a marriage license. Suddenly it all seemed to come together in my head. I liked David. He wanted to marry me. And, what the heck, I had to get to California.

Columnist Lee Mortimer announced the news: "The soon-to-be-married Copa chorines, Peggy Kohane to Gurney Munn, Jr. of the Social Register…Jessica

Barber to Eugene O'Neill, Jr...Harriet Weber to screen writer David Lord. The girls are leaving behind the luxury apartment they shared. Harriet, who was a World's Fair Aquacade starlet, is off to Hollywood to swim in the new Ester Williams film, *Bathing Beauties.*"

So with Terri as our witness, David and I were married at City Hall. My time at the world-famous Copa was memorable, but now I was going to work in another magical world: movies. Carrying not much more than pin money, I climbed aboard the train and joined my new husband as we chugged off into the Sunset—or in this case, the sunrise. We moved westward and I began to daydream. I would get to swim again, and visions of Eleanor Holm and Johnny Weissmuller danced before my eyes. What new adventures, what new people would I meet in Hollywood? Would I become famous in the movies, live in Hollywood or get a mansion with the Beverly Hills crowd? Would I get my footprints in front of Grumann's Chinese Theatre? I had all these crazy thoughts, and even though I was quick to remind myself that they were fantasy, nothing else, I couldn't help dreaming.

We happy honeymooners had a roomette aboard the train, while Terri had gone on ahead of us some day's earlier and would be staying at my sister Needy's place in Los Angeles. Miles past. I gawked at the scenery and David read or worked. We spent some time in bed, of course, but he wasn't any raving sex maniac. I kept having these conflicted feelings—sometimes ashamed that even though I liked David I was using him to get to California. Alternately, I felt I was entitled to do what I wanted as long as I didn't hurt anyone, and David seemed happy.

The trip took three days. I don't remember much about it, except for one little thing: for some reason, I took along my favorite childhood toy—a large doll with a bisque face. It was made in Germany and I received it as a Christmas gift when I was ten. It was sort of a good luck thing, a pacifying item I used to hug when I was nervous or uncertain. Why I knew I would need such an item, I don't know. Except perhaps, it was my first trip to California and my first stay in a moving room with a relative stranger to whom I had just committed myself. During the trip I got my first glimpse of his contradictory personality.

David was a quiet, soft-spoken kind of guy who kept things to himself. I didn't realize till later just how many things he did keep to himself. He was very amusing, for a while, because he knew so many funny stories about well-known people, like John Garfield because—I guess—he had told them so often, that they became a pattern for him. But, they grew tiresome after a few tellings. He gave the impression of being a laid back, know-it-all writer, but I began to realize later that he was as tense as a wound up mainspring, ready to pop at any minute. If he found himself at a dinner table facing the wall, he would become moody and refuse to eat. He tried to act cool and confident, but once I came to know him, I could see that the cool, like his stories, was a performance. In short, he was a shrink's delight.

The other side of his personality was fascinated by detail and how things worked. He did things carefully so he would do them correctly. He was careful not to get involved in things he could not control, and he would withhold a judgment or action until he was sure it was the right thing. But all of this is hindsight. At the time, I felt like the best-looking luckiest girl around. David doted on me, opened all the doors, held my coat, flattered consistently, in that thoughtful way he used when he wanted something. He was well read, cultured, good with details and patient. He was deliberate in his moves, but quick to analyze a situation. Now, after so many intervening years, I'm left with the impression of a carefully created show, hiding a man who didn't give much of himself away.

When we got to Los Angeles, David took me directly to his parent's home in the Valley near the studios, where we planned to stay until we found a home of our own. His father owned a barbershop in downtown Los Angeles, near city hall. For 40 years, he would say, he had cut the hair of all the big politicians and lawyers. To finish his script for the war training films, David went to work every day at Culver City, just a few miles down the road from his family home, but since I didn't drive, I was trapped in the house. Of course, I'd called Jimmy Durante as soon as we arrived and was waiting to hear back from him about auditions for the Ester Williams movie. I did get David to take me out frequently. That helped me get to know the city a little and to see some of the sights, which in the 1940's were as spectacular and exciting as the newsreels promised.

He had a good friend, an actor named Mark Lawrence, who, with his wife Sonya lived in the Hollywood hills in a house that seemed to me to be the quintessential actor's home: modern, spacious, cloaked in trees and shrubbery to ensure privacy, with a great view of the city. Everyone who likes old movies knows Mark Lawrence, even if they don't know his name. Every gangster movie of the 30's and 40's always seemed to have him as one of the bad guys, and just recently I saw him in "The Shipping News," where he played the cousin who lived in the hut by the water. He wasn't tall, but he had a mean look. He had steely eyes and a face marked by the small pox infection he had as a kid. He had a mean voice to go with that appearance, but that was all for the camera. On his own, at home with Sonya, he was a pleasant, soft-spoken man. I took to him right away, as I did to Sonya. Often we'd go there for cocktails before going out to dinner, and I always looked forward to it. This, I thought, was what it was like to be a Hollywood insider, especially, as it turned out, when another of David's friends happened to be Sydney Skolsky, the Hollywood gossip columnist.

He and his wife Estelle were also good friends of Mark's, and the first time we met them Mark was present when David introduced me as his wife. Mark waited for a lull in the conversation to ask, "How many wives do you have, David?" Nobody laughed. Nobody said anything. My antenna went up and at the first opportunity I confronted David as to what that remark meant. He said that he had been married once before. Mark, he said, knew he was separated, but not aware that he had gotten a divorce. I asked her name. "Ginger Kriter," he said, probably thinking I would leave it at that. But I didn't. I called every Kriter listed in the Los Angeles area phone book—and finally found her, still using David's name. For some reason, I wanted to meet her in person. Maybe because he had never revealed to me he had been married, I was now curious. The instinct must have been mutual because Ginger agreed immediately. We met in front of Mays department store in downtown Los Angeles and I spotted her right away. She looked a lot like me: same kind of figure and facial expressions. David's taste in women clearly ran to a type. And she had a little surprise for me: she and David filed for a divorce, but it wasn't final yet—it had two months to run. Two months? Then he must have known while he was in New York that he couldn't legally marry me.

I confronted David and he admitted he'd deceived me. So, I decided right there on the spot that I would get the marriage annulled. Actually, it was a great relief—I could part from him easily, since to some extent I'd made a marriage of convenience. In the meantime, I continued to live with his parents, and David and I actually managed to have some sort of social life together. But there was something more important on the horizon than disentangling myself from David—the movies! Jimmy had called back, and told me when to show up at the MGM studios.

The MGM lot, which was southwest of Hollywood and Vine, in a huge area called Culver City, was the most fabled of the big studios. Louis B. Mayer, who ran it, was the ultimate movie mogul. Many of the major movie stars of the era were under his contract, and he watched over them like a strict schoolteacher. Other studios—Paramount, Universal, Columbia, Warner Brothers, United Artists, Republic and a host of smaller ones—were also sprinkled throughout other parts of the city, like little kingdoms. MGM had its exclusive home along Washington Avenue.

Images of Hollywood always include the star's arrival by limousine, but I started more humbly. Since I didn't have a car, I walked. I identified myself with MGM's gatekeeper, and he said, "Here's your pass. Miss Weber." I felt a tingle run through me while those words rang in my ear. I was a little nervous, but also excited to be on the grounds of a real Hollywood studio. I was ready to prove myself to Esther Williams. I followed the directions to one of the many enormous buildings on the lot. Behind it was a giant in-ground pool, 90-feet square. I was told to see the wardrobe person inside, who gave me some forms to fill out, fitted me with a tank bathing suit, told me where to change, and left me with a gang of other girls. On Broadway, they would call this a cattle call, if the term applies to swimmers.

It took hours; as each swimmer was put through a series of moves to see how well she could swim. Even though I hadn't been swimming recently, almost a year, all the moves came back to me and managed to execute some of the intricate formations we did in the Aquacade, and generally just frolicked around, making sure my appraiser could see I was very much at home in the water. After I did my turn for a few moments, the stage manager told me to come out of the water, which I did with an acrobatic flair. I felt pretty confident until I noticed maybe a hundred girls doing the same thing! I did make the cut however, and was told the times and dates that rehearsals would start.

As I was leaving, I asked the stage manager standing around if Esther Williams was there. Not really understanding the Hollywood audition process I assumed that she'd be making the decisions! He gave me a look, as if to say, "how naïve are you?" I guess she wasn't. No matter, I wouldn't have recognized her anyway; I didn't even know what see looked like.

CHAPTER 10

On The Road Again

Even if I didn't get to meet the star, I was still young and green and thrilled to be in the entertainment business again, doing something I could do well. Maybe I'd be noticed, maybe singled out for a solo or something spectacular. After all, this was Hollywood, the land of fairy tales, and some fairy tales come true. I was here, wasn't I? Terri, with whom I would be sharing an apartment, had also auditioned successfully for yet another production of Peter Pan. We had dinner nearly every evening with my sister Needy and her husband, for which we were grateful, not just for her company, but also because it saved us some money. We didn't make much. My pay at MGM would only be $50 a week, and Terri was getting even less. So Needy was a Godsend. Starry eyed, I carried my good news home to my sisters, but reality set in the first day of shooting; I wouldn't get to be a star and the work was grueling.

We had to be there at 7 a.m. There were thirty beautiful swimmers in perfect sequences, and about a dozen chorus girls who were to move around the outside of the giant pool or stand on platforms—like the classic stage chorus designs that had been popular since the Ziegfeld Follies. The non-swimmers were all tall and stately, and probably models, because they knew how to stand and walk with that certain flair. Their costumes were net suits, large picture hats heavily decorated with flowers, and wedge shoes to accentuate their long legs. We swimmers wore scanty bodysuits—practical but sexy—and bathing caps decorated with flowers. John Murray Anderson, the same person who directed the Aquacade in New York City, would be directing the water sequences. There was another Aquacade connection: the star, Esther Williams, had starred in the San Francisco company of the Aquacade, where she was discovered and cast for this movie.

As so many movie performers discover when they get their first job in Hollywood, shooting a movie is tedious for everyone involved, cast and crew.

It's not like the stage, where performing live you have but one chance per performance to do it right or screw it up; where you can give your all to that one performance. In film you have dozens of chances to do it right (or wrong) and sometimes it takes that many run-throughs, sometimes more, before the director is satisfied. Whatever adrenaline you have pumping at the start is hard to maintain. If you are swimming, executing intricate maneuvers in a precisely timed rhythm, you get tired. We did this for seven weeks, resulting in about 10 minutes of footage that appeared in the movie.

One thing that never appeared while we were working was the star, Esther Williams. Her sequences were shot separately from ours, all except two long shots where she (or a double, I couldn't tell, because they didn't always tell us what exactly was happening) dove into the water while we were bobbing around, but not too close, to her. I did see her once or twice in between takes, just standing around, looking positively regal, with that famous smile and that beautiful figure. With her five-foot seven, 129 pounds frame, she was a natural princess. I wish we could have worked directly with her, all of us swimming together as we used to do with Eleanor Holm. But this was Hollywood. Everything was broken into small segments and photographed separately. Close-ups in and out of the water, medium shots with some swimmers, and then long shots that let the movie audiences admire all the stunning sets and scenery and the water pageantry as it unfolded. That long-shot pageantry was our contribution: the 30 soggy-but-hardy girls who swam through all the ballet sequences, with classical music blaring in the background so we could swim in syncopated precise formations.

We rehearsed for hours under hot lights with cameras rolling, stop and go, do it again, places again for a new camera setup—until John Murray finally got the mix of close-ups, long-shots, underwater, bird's eye views, and other sequences that he wanted. I was used to the repetitions of rehearsing, but the level of this grueling routine was new to me (and most of the other swimmers). When these shooting days ended, usually around 7 p.m., I would stagger home every night, where Terri and I would have dinner and I would collapse.

When my job was done and the thirty of us received our final paychecks I was truly glad. I felt it was time to move on. Throughout the shooting I kept in touch with Jimmy, who was filming on another lot. He used his influence to get me a job as a dancer in Marcel LaMaze's Clover Club, on the Strip at Sunset and La Cienega in West Hollywood. It reminded me a lot of Ben Marden's Riviera in New Jersey. The clientele were screened. The club's location was private, reached by driving up an incline flanked by palm trees, which hid the building from Santa Monica Boulevard below. The Clover Club was known as a private, members-only club and lots of stars continually passed through.

People came to eat and see a modest floor show. There was more talent in the audience than on the dance floor, where I was one of a half-dozen dancers who shuffled through some not-too-complicated routines in between the featured acts. The club closed at 2:00 AM. I spent more time with Jimmy, and his manager, Jack Roth, during this engagement than I ever had in New York, mostly because it was permitted to join them between shows, as it hadn't been at the Copa. Despite his outsized persona, Jimmy was a regular down-to-earth guy who just liked to help people. Sadly, people always assume that the casting couch is the only way girls got anywhere in show business. I'm happy to report that with me and Jimmy, that wasn't the case—we were, literally, "just good friends."

Jimmy lined up other work for me including a one-week stint as an extra on the Gene Kelly-Deanna Durbin film, Christmas Holiday. I also did a brief bit on Jack Benny's radio program as one of two telephone operators, either Brenda or Cobina, I forgot which, but it was great fun.

Despite these jobs and a few others, the dream of Hollywood had already soured for me. It seemed to me a city of desperate phonies. I was tired of the landscape, the same people obsessed with making movies, starring in them, or driving a new car or any of the other hang-ups that I found in most of the people I met there. But before I could clear out I had to deal with David. He had tried to persuade me to stay with him (and his domineering mother) until he could legally marry me, but I said no. David was one of the false things in Hollywood that I wanted to get away from. I was ready to go to Las Vegas to get the marriage annulled after I finished the swimming and had earned some additional money at the Clover Club. But, suddenly, I had another problem: I discovered I was pregnant.

I was so determined not to have a child with David, or to even be around him, that I decided to have an abortion. I searched the telephone book for a doctor nearest our house, and paid him a visit. Remember that this was the 1940s when such things weren't done openly. The doctor instructed me not to tell anybody about our meeting, and return the next day with $250.00. I remember thinking that his office looked a little shabby and dirty, and it was small, with only a table and a chair in it. But, I was so anxious to have it done and get it over with that these warning signals didn't register then. Upon my return I was to learn that he had never performed the procedure before: I was to be his test case!

I remember being "put under," yet feeling some horrible pain, and then there was a blank. I woke up in a hospital, hemorrhaging badly. I called David, not telling him why I was there and he came quickly, his mother with him. When they learned what had happened they were frightened because of the legalities, I guess, being that the marriage had not yet been annulled. Their concern about my health seemed minimal. Still, they took me home to recover. I was bedridden and in pain for the next two days. After a week I still couldn't stand up straight. I did heal, after a period of time (long after I had left David's mother's house). But there were after-effects that plagued me all my life. Looking back, while I could blame David for some of it, perhaps—if he were truly single and honest with me, who knows what I would have done when I discovered I was pregnant—I know I should have gotten better care to deal with the botched abortion. But somehow I couldn't stand the idea of other people knowing about this mess I created in my life.

When I was well enough to do things normally, Terri and I headed for Las Vegas, the only place in the country you could get a "fast" divorce or annulment in those days. Somehow we killed six weeks waiting for the annulment to go through, exploring the city and haunting the casinos. David called me frequently, but the old charm didn't work anymore: I wasn't having any of that "come back, all is forgiven" business. Sometimes we would just talk about our day's routine. I was always willing to talk to him while in Las Vegas, where time passes at a snail's speed. The only alternatives were cheap luncheonettes and Bugsy Siegel's casino, and gambling never appealed to me. Though, sometimes, I did enjoy watching the high rollers play.

In time I got over David, even to the point where I could see him and not get angry or teary-eyed. We even began an infrequent pattern of having dinner together and found we could tolerate, even enjoy one another's company for an evening. We continued this pattern later in life, but, as much as he hoped something serious would develop again, it never did. I had moved beyond the David Lords of this world—smooth talking to conceal dishonesty.

Perhaps the charm of Los Angeles had also worn off because I wasn't doing anything glamorous there, and I had the feeling I never would in that city. Terri's Peter Pan engagement had ended, and she was experiencing the same feeling. But, we were broke again, and trains or busses were expensive. The hatcheck girl in the Clover Club had an idea: "Look in the parking lots of expensive clubs and restaurants for autos with east coast license plates, and leave a note on the windshield requesting a ride. Why spend good money on travel? This was wartime; everyone seemed to be hitchhiking—riding with someone who happened to be going where you wanted to go, who would appreciate the company: driving solo being such a tedious affair. Everyone was doing it," she said.

When I told Terri, she thought it was a good idea too, and maybe if we got the right rides, we could do some sightseeing. But first, where to go? New York? No, we both agreed. We had come to like the warm climates and since this was the year 1941, the economy was booming and we felt we could get a job anywhere. But, just to be sure, I asked Jimmy if he could help. If I went to Miami, he said, I was guaranteed a job at the Clover Club there. That settled it. We were going to Miami, and we were going to get a free ride.

Today, of course, no one except the desperate or the naive solicits rides in a strangers' automobile. But during the war, public service messages encouraged people with cars to help other travelers, especially servicemen. After basic training, servicemen were given brief furloughs so they could return home for a few days before going overseas. So picking up hitchhikers became fairly common. In late 1941 that group included Terri and me. We were sure most male drivers would stop for pretty girls. (Remember Claudette Colbert in *It Happened One Night?*)

We went on a search, and sure enough we found a big Cadillac with Florida plates. I wrote a note explaining our need and including our phone number and stuck it under the windshield wiper. The next day, a guy called who said that he owned the Caddy, and yes, he was going to Florida in a few days and would be glad for our company. Success! On our first try! We congratulated ourselves on the shrewd strategy, and rewarded ourselves with a shopping spree. With our transportation worries behind us we loaded up on clothes, accessories and new luggage to carry all our earthly goods. When we got through, we had eight overstuffed bags. Our "ride" called the next day, as promised, but with bad news. His business was not yet concluded, and he didn't know when he would be, and couldn't leave town. We were disappointed but not discouraged.

It worked once it'll work again. We found another big car, a Buick, with Florida plates. Again we placed the note under the windshield wiper, again the return call, and again the commitment to take us along. To agree on plans, we set up a meeting at my older sister Needy's place, where her husband Arty could check out the driver. He turned out to be an older man (50 maybe?), heavyset with a thick Russian accent. He was quiet and didn't seem like the lecherous type. We agreed that Terri and I would split expenses on gas and food, and that we'd pay for our own motel accommodations. So all agreed, we settled on a travel date and said goodbye.

The day we were to leave, like all California days, dawned bright and sunny, and we arrived at curbside at the designated time. The Buick pulled up; the driver emerged, took one look at our mountain of luggage and nearly fell over. Our eight bags were somehow crammed into the trunk and back seat, and the three of us sat in front with Terri in the middle, and off we went. After about an hour's drive, the roaming fingers began. Terri was nearest, so she got most of it, but I got a little. Twist, slap and yell as we did, nothing seemed to deter him for long. He didn't argue or say anything. He'd just wait a few moments and then start again. We, being wedged in, could do little expect push away his right hand. Fortunately he kept his left hand on the wheel. Finally, Terri bit his hand and he yowled and pulled back. We told him to quit, and he didn't say anything, but for the most part gave his hand a rest. We knew we'd never last a full trip with this guy, but we also knew that we couldn't leave him the first night; the first stop would be some little town in Arizona. Since it was clear that we weren't going to let him grope us all the way across the country, we considered the possibility that this guy would probably like nothing better than to strand us in the desert. We needed to be ready.

As night fell, without asking us or saying much of anything, he pulled into a motel on the outskirts of a small town and we registered in separate rooms. An hour or so later we went back to the desk clerk and prepaid the night's lodging. If our driver was going to depart unexpectedly, we were going to be ready. We took turns staying up to keep watch while the other got some sleep, knowing we'd need it if we were to get back into that car with him. His hands would be well rested by morning.

At 5:00 a.m. we took our bags outside and arranged them in the driveway. Sure enough, about 5:30 our driver came slowly out of his cabin. (He must have prepaid, too!) When he reached the driveway exit, there were our eight bags blocking the way and the two of us sitting atop them. "Ready to go?" we asked cheerfully. He fumed, silently, but let us stow our bags as before. We made room for Terri in the back seat and I sat as close to the side window as I could. He'd need octopus arms to reach us now. But we'd obviously spoiled his fun. He didn't even attempt anything. We drove in silence. Still, Terri and I were determined that this would be our last day in this car.

Checking into a modest hotel in El Paso, we were delighted knowing we would finally part company from our driver. The owner of the hotel was an ex-showgirl. We became friends instantly, especially when we told her about the "roving hands" experience. When the driver came into the lobby and saw how well Terri and I were getting along with her, he started badmouthing us saying how awful we were, giving him such a hard time as he was doing us a favor by taking us with him, and so on. "I can always call my friend at the police station to sort it out for you," she said. "Of course…he may arrest you for transporting a minor across state lines." That shut him up pretty quick, and before long he got in his car and pulled off. Great! We've seen the last of him! Feeling a little vengeful, I mentioned that he was carrying stolen Army T-coupons, which I saw when he was buying gas. In fact, he bragged about having them and how important that made him. The hotel owner gleefully called in this bit of information to the local police, who (we were to learn later) apprehended him on the road. We thought nothing more about it.

As a border town there was no shortage of cars or drivers in El Paso. But realizing we were true greenhorns about hitchhiking, our new friend decided to give us some helpful tactics about getting rides. The trick, she said, was to not give a driver a reason to pass you by. For instance, when standing on the road awaiting traffic, have only two bags next to you. Hide the rest behind a bush or a sign. Then when someone stops, one person can hold the front door open (as if preparing to get in the car) while the other loads the other bags into the back seat or trunk. Don't ask, just do it. Never accept a lift with someone who's traveling less than 100 miles further on. And, always have a map, so you can see how far you'll be from a good-sized town or city when you stop for the night.

Later that afternoon we were sitting in the cocktail lounge when two Navy lieutenants (that were staying in the same hotel) invited us to dinner. After our ordeal with the fat Buick man we could use a distraction, and accepted. Next thing we knew we found ourselves in a car heading across the Mexican border to Juarez. There, in an intimate rooftop restaurant, we dined and danced. What a wonderful spontaneous moment. One of the two was getting married in a few days, and we were invited to the wedding. After a brief huddle, we said we'd love it. They made arrangements for us to stay at the Navy Officers Club and we spent the next few days sightseeing and eating at the club on base or in little cute restaurants. The wedding was a happy occasion, a great party, and the beginning of a pen-pal friendship that lasted for years. That was another thing bout the war: with so much uncertainty about the future, the present was lived at an accelerated pace.

The day after the wedding, one of the Navy drivers dropped us off at the highway and we were on our own, glad to be moving again, and wiser for all we had experienced so far. We followed our hotel owner's guidelines faithfully. When the first car stopped, I engaged in small talk, holding the passenger door open, while Terri heaved the luggage into the back seat. This always seemed to work from then on. We'd always smile, and in effect, never give them a chance to protest our eight suitcases. And by asking sweetly, we'd always get our own way. We learned some other useful tricks too, beginning with our first ride of the day. After the bags were stowed, we'd ask our driver (always a man) if he could stop at the next roadside place for breakfast. The driver would usually offer to pay for our breakfasts even before we stopped. So we'd stuff ourselves with eggs, bacon, ham, rolls, whatever, so we wouldn't be hungry if we were on the roadside without the opportunity to eat lunch later in the day. From El Paso on, we never paid for a meal. Highway travelers that we had become, we paid our way with our stories about how and why we were hitchhiking; relating some of our experiences. We had enough stories to last a couple of hours, at least—almost everyone was curious.

More than once we noticed that cars would sail right past a serviceman who was hitchhiking and then stop for us. So we decided that any driver who stopped for us had to take the serviceman as well. Sometimes a driver would balk at that, but we were insistent. If the serviceman couldn't be brought along, we wouldn't go. We never met a driver who resented our attitude once we were all aboard and moving. (We secured rides for several servicemen on that trip.)

We met a lot of people who were nice to us during that week on the road, but no one was more grateful for our company than the truck drivers. They loved to bring us into the truck-stop diners and restaurants and show us off. Our stories kept them entertained and most gave us their addresses—imploring us to let them know how we fared. We always felt safe, and traveling with them was a nice change of pace. Sometimes it was fun to ride in the back of an open truck, catching the breeze and sampling the goods the truck was carrying, especially if it was fresh fruit or vegetable, chocolates, cakes, cookies or watermelon. There I was roaring along an interstate, my back against the truck's forward wall, eating a banana and watching the scenery unfold around me. It was one of those in-the-moment experiences that I could never have planned for.

After an extended stay on a roadside without catching a ride, we attracted the attention of five marines riding in an old car. We wanted to get somewhere for the evening, so even though it seemed a bit risky and was against our rules (to get in a car with several men), we climbed aboard. For 500 miles we had the best time, singing and joking all the way: one of them had a guitar, another a harmonica. The time and miles flew. They were all AWOL as it turned out, and would catch hell when they got back to base, but right now they didn't care. The ending was fittingly unexpected. They ran out of gas. I have sometimes wondered what happened to those five crazy guys. Though at that time we were just determined to keep going and returned to the highway, seeking another ride.

While God may have rested on the seventh day, we didn't. We were still traveling and had only reached Palm Beach Florida, still an hour or so from our final destination. So it was back to the roadside again, our eight bags and us. We noticed a little car with rumble seat—which sort of folded up out of where the truck would be—approaching, but there were three servicemen in it; a lieutenant was driving. When they stopped we explained that we appreciated the offer, but we wouldn't get in a car with three guys. We figured we had come this far without any mishaps and weren't going to screw up now. But two of the guys said they could walk to where they were going. So, when they got out, we happily got in. The driver, a cute blonde fellow, drove on and asked where we were going. "Miami," we said.

Don Ruffin Tisdall was an army pilot, and told us he was only going as far as the base in Boca Raton where he was stationed, but would be happy to take us that far. "By the way, what's in it for me by giving you lift?" he asked. I snapped, "You ought to be ashamed of yourself. You're a disgrace to the army!" He shot back, "Only for her. I never would have stopped for you." It was an uncompromising beginning to an event that would have reverberating results. When our ride came to an end, our driver, clearly smitten with Terri asked for our address and phone number. Without hotel arrangements, we told him "general delivery, Miami." We said goodbye and he pulled off. One ride later we arrived in Miami Beach.

We checked into the Westview, a small hotel on the bay, and it was such a

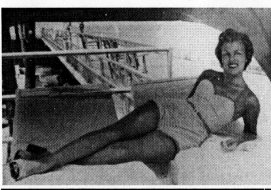

Harriet—1943

relief to finally arrive. The hotel had a nice atmosphere, with other young people down for the season (November—March), working at all sorts of odd jobs around the city. We slept well and relaxed for the next day or so, before I started at my job at the Clover Club. The dance routines were like the ones I'd performed at the Sunset Strip club, so I fit in quickly.

Terri found a job as a checker at the Roney Plaza Hotel, and we easily slipped back into a day-to-day lifestyle. It was good to earn a living again.

CHAPTER 11

An Unexpected Twist

Several weeks later there was a knock at our door. When I opened it there stood our pilot from Boca Raton asking for Terri. He had been writing to her and I had been answering, though he thought it was Terri because in my letters I didn't set him straight. She wasn't interested in him, but I was, so I had been hoping that he would show up. He was a tall, rangy guy with a nice smile and an easy manner. He was also young—24 (I was 22) and like many servicemen, especially pilots, living only for today.

Our first date came about because he eventually saw that he would get nowhere with Terri, especially when he learned that she was only 16 years old—he gulped at the news. So he asked me out. I was concerned that his being a handsome pilot probably made him accustomed to getting his way with girls, but I went out with him anyway. After dinner, as soon as he parked the car, he was all over me. I pushed and shoved him away, but he was determined. Finally, I kicked him in the legs (the car space being what it was I couldn't kick him where I wanted to), bit him and spat in his face. That slowed him down enough so that I could get out of the car. I walked out to the street and he called out to me telling me to "wait a minute." His expression was exasperation and regret. He begged me not to leave the parking lot, saying that he'd be good, and insisted over and over that he was sorry.

I wasn't buying it. I told him never to call again. As far as I was concerned, that was that. I told Terri about it when I got home and she was sympathetic because she sensed that I really liked the guy. I've been around lots of men who thought because I was a showgirl, or because I ran with a fast crowd in New York or LA, that I was a pushover. That's not so. I have never sought or enjoyed casual sex. In the forties, very few girls like me, brought up in neighborhoods like mine, by parents like mine, had premarital sex. We might have fooled around a bit, and there surely were girls who gave a preview to hasten a marriage proposal. But for me (and most others, I believe) going steady didn't mean going to bed together. Sex to me was part of love.

Of course, everyone thinks of those wartime love stories the movies are so fond of, where a girl in love with a serviceman gives him whatever he wants because in war a girl never knows if her man will return. But in real life most of these couples at least preceded the occasion with a quickie marriage. I know that today's sexual mores came about not by a change in religion or ethics or whatever, but because of changing attitudes about contraceptives. The point is, most couples that fell in love in my days did follow rules, and we didn't consider them overly strict. Men who wouldn't respect those rules, and the boundary lines we drew, were usually sent packing.

So, Don went back to Boca Raton and I thought the episode was behind me. But he didn't, and continued to write. We didn't answer. I say "we" because some of the letters were addressed to me, and some to Terri; he was either still attracted to her or wanted to reach me through her. After a few weeks of this, Terri and I were getting ready to go to work one evening, when a knock came at the door. I opened it and Don was standing there. I tried to slam the door shut but he stuck his foot in it. "Truce," he said. "Let's start all over. I promise to be a gentleman and behave." He went on to say that army life had gotten the better of him. Moreover, he finalized realized that it was I who had been writing the letters to him, and that it was the writer of those letter—me—he wanted to be with.

I didn't quite believe him, but he had been so persistent that I was willing to give him another chance. And at that point he seemed willing to devote himself to me. Later that week he came to the Clover Club to watch me (and seven girls with big pink hats) dance, and when I looked across the room and saw him, my whole heart turned over. It was at dinner that night that I began to know the real Don. We talked about family and dreams. He was the youngest of 15 children. His parents were from Bergen, Norway, and had settled years before in Minot, North Dakota, where many Swedes and Norwegians had established themselves. No wonder he was a hustler, I thought, to get any attention when you're one of 15 you have to be aggressive. As he revealed more and more of himself, little by little, I came to really like him. I could see that he liked me, and he said he had since we first met. After that night our relationship blossomed, and after only six dates he asked me to marry him. I said no. I wasn't ready. But I was pleased to be asked. So we continued to date and my love for him grew. We would meet in Fort Lauderdale whenever we could, usually on Thursday nights. Sometimes we stayed up so late I'd miss the last bus back to Miami and stay with him for the night. We'd both leave early the next morning, and he had to hurry to get back to the base on time.

When we were apart, he wrote me mad love letters, increasingly passionate and urgent. In one sentence he'd threaten to stop seeing me if I didn't marry him, and in the next he'd say I was the only thing that mattered to him. He was miserable when we were apart. I must admit that I was too. He always questioned whether I loved him as much as he loved me, seeming to need to be reassured that I wouldn't leave him. Still I hesitated. I had a life of my own and I wasn't sure I wanted to give up being in show business to become a wife and mother. And that was one of his fears—that our lifestyles were too different; that I was too much into the glamour of show business and a busy and varied social life.

I came to realize that before Don I had never loved before. Our sex life was fabulous, and he taught me things I had never known about love and intimacy. I experienced for the first time such things as taking a shower together, and undressing before one another (rather than separately in the closet or the bathroom). He made me promise that I would never fake an orgasm, like many girls did. We spoke of things that were new to me, and he was not afraid to reveal his emotions. The frankness and honesty in the way he spoke of such things touched me in a way I had never before experienced. For the first time in my life I understood what it was like to love and be loved. We would say to each other, again and again, that being together was all that mattered. I admitted to myself that deep down in my heart I wanted to marry him. But, I still didn't know what to do with the other elements of my life. But I would have to make a decision soon; Don's training was due to end very soon, and he would be reassigned to some other base.

As it had happened before in my life, and would happen again, an unexpected circumstance settled the matter. I was on stage dancing at the Clover Club. In the audience, as usual, I saw the club owner, Mr. Friedlander. We had always gotten along OK, and why not, since Jimmy Durante had recommended me. Just then I saw an old, fat guy stroll into the club and walk over to the owner's table. He looked familiar some how. Suddenly it dawned on me: that's the dirty old man in the Buick, the one with the roaming hands, that guy we sent the cops after. After the last show, the owner called me over. I was told to go upstairs where he had an apartment, and wait. Being no dummy and having seen a few things in this business, I assumed this Buick guy—who clearly knew Friedlander—wanted some payback, probably in bed. I promptly refused. I was just as promptly fired on the spot. Effective immediately.

I was distraught. Even though I had heard about such things with other girls, I never thought it would happen to me. My first thought was to call Jimmy to see if he could help, but then it occurred to me, to what end? Even if Jimmy could get my job back, there would still be uneasiness there. This Buick guy, who lived in Florida and clearly had influence with Friedlander, would always prove a danger to me. I called Don and poured out the whole story. He said he'd drive to Miami to get me. He played down the importance of my humiliation saying it would pass and those guys weren't worth any embarrassment. What was important, he continued, was that our life together could finally begin; "we'll get married tonight!" I told him that I wanted him to meet my family first. "No," he said, "I'm not marrying your family I'm marrying you! It's tonight or never!" I hesitated. I didn't say yes, and after a short silence, he said goodbye and hung up.

I was really heartbroken now, but knew I couldn't just run off and get married like that. When Terri heard the story, she said, "let's go home." We felt a little nervous calling Ben in New York because we hadn't parted on very cordial terms. He must have missed us though, because he wired us money for airfare, arranged an apartment for us in the Beaux Arts Hotel on East 44th Street in Manhattan, and even called my older sister Needy in California to have her come to New York and help us resettle. At that moment I was so proud of Ben, and grateful too.

Rather than fly, we decided to save some of the money and rely on our now-familiar method of travel—hitchhiking. However, no eight-bag traveling this time, we sent all but one bag ahead. The rides we got were uneventful and that was just as well. We used the time to map out our next steps. Don's name never came up in conversation although I thought about him all the time, trying to convince myself that it wouldn't be the end of the world if my decision to not elope broke us up. But deep down I knew if anything spoiled what we had for one another I'd never recover. For now, I'd just have to wait till we spoke to see how he felt. Three days later we arrived in Manhattan.

Several weeks after we settled into the Beau Arts Hotel—about a month after Don hung up on me—Ben got a telegram. It was from Don. He would be arriving at Newark Airport at 2:00 a.m. and requested that we meet him. My two sisters went with me. When his flight landed at the army airstrip and I saw his familiar figure come strolling across the field, I thought I would melt. By the expression on his face I knew in that instant we would get married. My heart sang! We stayed up the rest of the night, making plans and talking about our future. It was a glorious feeling. Everything again was new, exciting, and the future seemed bright. The next morning he met Ben, who was probably irritated because he wasn't consulted about our plans. "Why, you're just a pissy-assed kid in the army." Don remained calm. "I didn't come here to ask you if we could get married, but to tell you. All we want are your good wishes." Ben's feathers were clearly ruffled, but he backed off and wished us well.

Don tried to get a leave right away but couldn't swing it. These were critical times and he was needed back on base immediately. A hurricane was brewing in the Caribbean and all pilots were being called in to get the planes off the field and moved to safety in other parts of the country. So our engagement lasted three months. We were married on May 29, 1944 in Palm Beach in the judge's chambers at City Hall. Ben and Bea came down for the Ceremony, though my sisters couldn't make it. We spent the next few weeks in our apartment near the base in Boca Raton (Married couples were required to live off base), and took most of our meals at the Officers Club (in a building that is the Boca Raton Club today.)

Another reason for acting so quickly once we decided to wed was Don's postings. We had to be ready to move on a moments notice. We never had the time for a formal honeymoon, but in a sense we didn't need one. Everything was new. We were honeymooners for months. I was learning how to cook, something I never had to do before. As a child, my mother took charge of that and didn't do any teaching, not that I would have been willing student. Later, during my days at the Copa and later in California, I always ate out, usually at fine places where someone else picked up the tab. In short I was spoiled because I knew what great meals tasted like, and now I had to learn to prepare them! Don was patient, and eventually I developed a flair for cooking.

We traveled courtesy of Uncle Sam and Don's assignments took us to Colorado, Texas, California, Florida and one memorable tour of duty—Clovis, New Mexico. Memorable because that's where I gave birth to our child. It was night, and contractions started without much warning. Don helped me to the car and we headed for the hospital. From what seemed like out of nowhere rose a violent dust storm. Visibility was zero, and I feared that I would have to give birth in the car. Don struggled to see, and in panic drove blind for quite a while. By accident, or luck, just as the tension was sky high, we found the hospital and the birth occurred without further incident. We were the proud parents of a healthy boy who I named Clovis, after the town in which he was born. Nowadays people are named after towns or countries (such as Paris, America, Dakota, Africa, etc.) all the time, but back then it wasn't quite so common. More so because it was a place that few—if any—had ever heard of. Years later when he was grown, Clovis asked me what he would have been named if he was born in a place that didn't lend itself to a child name, like Pork Chop, Idaho. The truth is I don't know what I would have named him in that case, though I told him, "Simple, I would have named you "Porky." I was kidding, of course.

I learned to like Army life and over the next few months learned how to cook, sew and do laundry. Despite that there was not much to do there everything was new to me, and for that reason life in general was an adventure. I became active in the USO and found some creative outlet in designing and constructing costume jewelry. With all the new things I was learning, the one that I failed at miserably was learning to drive. Being blind in one eye, my eyesight was poor from the start, and to make matters worse I had no depth perception. The first time I tried to move the car I backed it into a tree. I didn't get much better either. In time I'd drive to do errands, but that was really an adventure. Driving frightened me, and often I found myself involuntarily closing my eyes when I passed another car, or they passed me! This had many results; driving into a ditch and needing the wrecking truck pull me out was one, and on many more occasions driving to the auto repair shop was the other.

Don didn't realize how bad a driver I was. I didn't want to tell him because I didn't want him to spend all his free time—he had so little of it—driving me around the base for my errands. But he was bound to find out sooner or later. And he did. One evening when he came home, he greeted me in the kitchen by saying, "In the dark, I can see a fresh paint job. No more driving for you." To this day, I haven't driven since. Time passed quickly. A new life, and new places filled my days. On our first wedding anniversary, Don was away on a mission, and he sent this telegram:

> One year with the wrong woman is more than
> a man can stand. But one year with you is
> more than I'm entitled to. May the rest of my
> life be made up of such years!
> All my love, Don

Like many towns that became military centers during the war, makeshift accommodations were secured, and military people ended up with all kinds of oddball living quarters. Don and I ended up with an apartment over a garage. The landlady was a screwball, and if her son hadn't been a local policeman, she would have been locked up for sure. I'd do the laundry and hang the clothes in the backyard, and without a thought she'd go for the garden hose and soak everything. She'd sprinkle tacks in the driveway, and do dozens of other wacky things. She'd get in her car and drive it up and back in the driveway for hours, blowing the horn all the time—any time of the day or night. When Clovis was sleeping in the carriage seemed like an appropriate time (to her).

Don worked many irregular shifts, and her looniness was more than he should have had to deal with, but he was patient. We knew housing was tight, and at least we had a place all to ourselves, unlike other married couples in the service. After the war ended and we got our reassignment, Don got even. He paid the final month's rent in loose pennies and before we drove away for good, he cut up the clothesline into six-inch pieces. As we drove out of sight, we could see her raging, being consoled by her son, the policeman.

We were elated to be getting away from that crazy woman. But also because Don had been awarded a plush assignment—Cairo, Egypt. We were going to live abroad, assigned to the American Embassy. I couldn't believe it. Don was one of only twelve men selected (from over 1200) who took a special qualification exam for the Military Attaché Diplomatic Service. So I knew we'd get a nice position, maybe even New York or New Jersey instead of one of those desert villages out west where so many servicemen wound up. As it turned out he'd be flying VIPs all over the Middle East.

CHAPTER 12

Off We Go Into The Wild Blue Yonder

The end of World War II marked the beginning of a mad stampede by American servicemen to become civilians again. Because the military never does anything in a hurry, many GI's languished in their uniforms for months before they were processed out. For those who had jobs waiting for them, adjusting to civilian life was a pleasant task. Others had a rough time. Don and I had it easy because we had concluded long before that we would stay in the service. I had become accustomed to the transient life style of an army wife. Don loved to fly, and he was good at it. Army life for dependents had many attractions; government housing; living allowances; good schools; food and clothing. And, there was the feeling that because you're moving every few years that you're always on vacation.

December 3, 1946 we found ourselves aboard the USS Vulcania, leaving New York harbor for Cairo, with stops along the way in several Italian ports. Our ship was the first commercial ship to debark from New York since the war ended. Many of the other passengers were Roman Catholic priests on their way to Rome; to find their families and help with relief efforts, so we had a very spiritual (and eventful) voyage. It wasn't a luxury cruise. There were only about seventy-five passengers aboard, and most of the crew was prisoners-of-war now working their way home. I entertained the priests with jokes that—despite being a little off color—always seemed to get a laugh. The mood was light and friendly.

That all changed when we reached our first port of call, Naples. The famed city on Italy's west coast was one of the most damaged from the war, but few people were aware of that in those first postwar months—including the U.S government. As we approached, ships were half sunk, on their sides, littered throughout the harbor. They were casualties of war, like crimpled animals that had just recently been slain and left to die. As the ship neared the dock we all came up on deck. We could see throngs of people on the shore. Were they waiting to greet us? Were they coming aboard? No one seemed to know. We could hear them now. But, they weren't cheering or waving or acting anything like a welcoming committee. They were screaming, pushing and gesturing. They were a mob, angry and we didn't know why. We soon learned they were hungry—starving, in fact. Naples had virtually nothing left when the war ended. Bombs had destroyed many of the neighborhoods, and none of the stores were functioning. Even if they had been, there was nothing to buy, or money to buy it with. Kids and gangsters ran wild; it was an "open city." So when a huge ship steamed into Naples, the citizens turned out, hoping for some food or something they could sell on the Black Market.

The police fought a futile battle to keep the crowds away from the docks as they kept pushing against the police lines. It threatened to get ugly. They were yelling and cursing—you didn't need to speak Italian to understand their meaning. From the deck we watched it all unfold, wondering how all those priests would be able to disembark for their ride to Rome. Disobeying the orders to stay aboard, some passengers moved tentatively down the gangplank. The first of them who reached the dock were pounced upon as soon as they stepped on shore. Their clothes were literally torn off. It was not a pleasant welcome and we were frightened. Without warning the crowds burst through the police lines and stormed the gangplank. Some ship passengers shrank away from the rail and headed for the safety of places below deck. Emboldened by the gangplank invaders other Neapolitans scampered up the ship's ratlines and clung to the hull, trying to climb aboard that way. Finally, all the passengers were ordered back to their cabins for the night, while the officials tried desperately to restore order. It was a mad house. My first time in Europe and it had to be under martial law!

As Americans, we had been engaged in World War II; our soldiers fought throughout the South Seas and Europe, while the civilians at home were keeping our country's economy and manufacturing plants operating. We had listened to it on the radio, read about it in the newspapers, but it was all happening on a distant shore. Even today, many American's don't realize how close the war was to our back door. You can still see a German submarine beached in Acapulco Bay, and there were reports of German subs as close as the coast of Massachusetts. I lay in bed that night remembering a cold winter night while I was still working at the Copacabana. My girlfriend Jessica and I were doing the midnight "scramble" again, on a double date at a restaurant uptown on East 85th street and 3rd Ave. We ate and drank and had nice conversation.

After coffee one of the men said, "there's a private party in the back and I have to show up just for a minute." I smiled, "Private party, OK, let's go."

As we stepped into the small back room of the restaurant I was dumbfounded. I had stumbled down the rabbit hole and landed in a bad dream. I surveyed the room with my eyes and chills ran up and down my spine. My heart began to race and I was afraid. Nazi Swastikas hung on the wall; men in German uniforms were everywhere—I was horrified. This was New York City, early 1941, before America had even entered the war. I understood at that moment what it would have felt like for a colored person to mistakenly stumble into a KKK meeting. I didn't know what to do—my blood pressure was rising by the second. I thought for sure I would be spotted as an intruder, with who knows what consequences. I continued to force a smile, saying hello and acting friendly. I quietly leaned over to my date, "Jessica and I really have to get back for our next show…you stay, we'll grab a cab," and we darted out. I was frightened and knew something dangerous was brewing. I told Ben what happened, though to this day I don't know what he did, or didn't do about it. Until now I hadn't thought much about it.

The next morning our sightseeing experience in Naples had to be one of the saddest and most touching journeys in the history of "tourist" travel. It wasn't a city. It was a shambles, chaos personified. For the soldiers the war might have been over, but for the people here the war of survival was still underway. Our group was on foot, so we got an up-close look at the houses, apartment buildings and offices bombed out; they were mere shells. The streets wound around in confusing ways, made more so by all the destruction. Trolley cars ran where and when they could on some streets, while horse-drawn carriages served as taxis. Gasoline had run out months ago, even for military vehicles. I didn't see one working automobile in Italy.

Even churches had been bombed and their interiors gutted. Many buildings had no roofs, or sides, and their innards were exposed to anyone passing by. People had set up living areas where they could, often on the street, and being December it was cold. Broken furniture and household goods were everywhere. So were the people; shuffling along wearing threadbare clothing and on their feet, quite often slippers, shoes with holes, or nothing at all. Here and there you could see a touch of what was once beautiful. Some of the neighborhoods untouched by bombs looked modern and clean, for instance the new areas around the post office, one of Mussolini's (and the city's) proudest structures. Some looked like the buildings I had seen at the 1939 World's Fair. But outside those untouched buildings you still saw wretched poverty: kids in rags, and shoes without holes were a rarity. It was frightening and pitiful. The newsreels couldn't capture the sense of ruin we were presented with.

Strangely, the Italian tour guide who escorted us pretended that certain ugly things we saw just weren't there. Everybody seemed to know we were Americans. In what I imagine was a stupid moment I asked our guide if I was right about this, and he just looked at me. I hadn't realized how different we must have looked. Everywhere we went people hovered, following our group for a while as we walked up and down the battered streets looking at the destruction, most of it caused by American bombers and GI's in Italy's final days. Perhaps they thought we might throw them a coin, or give them something we were wearing. That thought crossed my mind, but I quickly remembered that such a simple gesture could set off an unwanted chain of events similar to the scene that unfolded at the dock the day before. I had the sense that these people didn't like us, that they resented our presence even though they didn't know why we were there.

Things looked better later on as we reached the suburbs, on our way to Mount Vesuvius and Pompeii. The landscape reminded me of California: ornate terracotta homes, groves of olive, orange, and lime trees. Goatherds, with the sound of their tinkley bells were ever present. The volcano was smoking that day, and dark sooty clouds hovered all during our stay there. The thought occurred to me that about the only thing that hadn't happened to Naples during World War II was a volcanic eruption. Then I was told that that had happened, too. The last eruption occurred in 1942, shortly after America entered the war. While we were there, we decided to see the ruins of Pompeii; the ancient city engulfed in volcanic lava in 79 A.D., which occurred so fast and furious, that life there was captured in time the split second that it ceased.

After seeing the ruin of Naples, Pompeii seemed almost calm and tidy. I was surprised to see that one of the best-preserved places inundated by Vesuvius' lava was a bordello. Not that I was shocked to see a bordello; my life hadn't been that sheltered. What did shock me however was to see such sexually explicit scenes. They were so well preserved, everything so vivid. Don was as fascinated as I was. I didn't think that whorehouses were treated as tourist attractions, although when I thought about it, I said, why not?

When we returned to the Vulcania we were informed that we had to stay aboard ship for the rest of the night. It wasn't safe to be ashore after dark because we'd be sitting ducks for those food-and-clothing-hungry Neapolitans. Desperate people would even jump into carriages to rob people as they rode by. To keep some sense of order, there were soldiers about, and in their black boots, they looked like Nazi caricatures.

The Italian Lira was now inflation bloated and virtually worthless. But merchandise? There was a black market for everything, cameras, jewelry, clothes, and especially American cigarettes, and its merchants weren't bashful. They'd buttonhole you in broad daylight and be persistent enough to make you push them out of your way. They liked to get heavy jewelry, cameos, anything old. Most of what was gotten eventually was traded away for the most basic staples—like food—which in turn would be a bargaining chip for something else. Such was the hand-to-mouth existence that one can't even imagine when we think of the glamour and style that characterizes today's Western Europe.

Since I had never been to Europe before, I was surprised to find that many of the Italians were fair-skinned, some with blue eyes and blonde hair. I presumed all Italians looked like the ones I saw in Brooklyn with that Al Pacino look. There were some of those as well, but it was the fair-complexioned Italian girls that made direct assaults on the young American officers who spent their day hours ashore. And the men were as eager for the girls as the girls were for them. For a young American officer who wasn't too lovesick for a girl back home to pay attention to the risks, it was a grand tour of duty. But those pretty girls were in the minority. Most Italians wore a haggard look, with sickly eyes and beaten-down postures. Begging was a common, if mostly futile, occupation, for both women, and men. All in all, Don and I were happy to get back to sea and on our way to Egypt.

Because of the danger of mines, this was no quick voyage. The ship had to take a zigzag route down the Italian coast, where we passed another volcano, Mount Stromboli, sitting out there in the middle of nowhere, surrounded by water. But finally, about 2:00 p.m. on a bright December day just before Christmas, we arrived at Alexandria, the ancient city where the Mediterranean meets the mouth of the Nile River. It took five hours to clear customs and get ashore, where the Army waited with five cars and two trucks. After the Embassy people (who were all civilians, not military like us) were sorted and shipped out, there were eight of us left: Don, Clovis, me; a couple from Tennessee, an Embassy official and his wife en route to Palestine, and General Schwarzkopf, the father of General Norman Schwarzkopf of Desert Storm fame. I wish I could say our families spent a lot of time together in Egypt, but we didn't. We never saw them again because we were the only ones continuing on to Cairo.

My first impression of Egypt was that I was in the land of slumber. Everyone was wearing what looked like long nightgowns and red fez hats with a tassel. Some of the men had garments wrapped around their legs and their pants hung down low. Everybody seemed to yell a lot, and wave his or her hands so vigorously that if you happened to get in the way, you'd be knocked down. Adding to these strange impressions, I was also convinced that everyone was cross-eyed, but was later told that there's so much dust and sand in the air, that the eye muscles can't function as they are supposed to.

Our small group was told to be careful and stay together because we had docked in a bad part of town. A long ride to Cairo awaited Don, Clovis and me as soon as the embassy car could get to us. For now, all we could do was wait and get a feel for these odd-looking people we would be living with for the next three years. It was a daunting thought. Even Don looked grim, and he always gave the impression that no matter what came along he could handle it. Eventually, our driver, carrying a gun, as did his companion (who rode most of the way on the running board, his weapon ready) arrived with the car. The concern was robbers, who preyed on vehicles on the road between Alexandria and Cairo.

CHAPTER 13

A Cold Night In Cairo

After riding through the bright white sand for two hours or so, we stopped for a meal. The place was an inn with a French menu. "Good," I whispered to Don. "I could eat a horse." He grinned, "Don't make any wishes out loud, they may come true." Instantly I envisioned camels being butchered for steaks. I ordered eggs. The meal was fine, especially the butter, which was made from goats' milk and was a pale pink color. The sugar looked and felt like coarse salt. All the while I kept my eye on the drivers because somewhere deep down inside I feared of what might happen if they decided to leave us stranded here. As far as I was concerned we were in the middle of nowhere, menaced by dark people in flowing robes who might do terrible things to white people, especially women and little boys. My ignorance—and vivid imagination—at work! Don, had recovered his spirits and was enjoying himself. The meal took a little longer than we expected because the guards ate separately to take turns watching the car. No matter how remotely you think you are situated, we were warned, there's always somebody ready to steal any vehicle left unattended.

Finally, we got underway again, and we tried to kill time by counting all the camels we saw. That game became tedious when it seemed like every sand dune had its own camel. A few more hours passed and we finally arrived in Cairo. It was late, so we only got a quick glimpse of the city. Our destination—a temporary one—was the elegant Shepherds' Hotel; the same one in which the Allied Big Three, Roosevelt, Churchill, and Stalin once met during World War II. Considering all the details that the military had to deal with to move its people where they were needed, it wasn't surprising when some things didn't happen on time. For our part, we not only fought the heat, but also a civil service system that did things in its own time and manner. In short, we had to adjust.

Our first adjustment was a temporary home because our apartment wasn't ready. Because everything seemed so new and exciting, I didn't mind any of the delays, as long as I had a place to eat and sleep, and I was with my family. Don had to get to work almost immediately, but he did find time to go to Alexandria to retrieve our belongings: trunks, clothes and Clovis's carriage and playpen, which we needed desperately. After being so long "en route," we were ready to settle down. Clovis and I began to have a grand time getting acquainted with this new city and a new culture. Before long, our permanent residence at 1 Sharia El Walda in the Garden City section of Cairo was ready. It was worth the wait!

The apartment was huge, with an impressive entrance hall, five bedrooms, living and dining rooms, a roof garden, and a room for the live-in nurse who tended to Clovis. The other two servants, called "safroggies," assigned to us to clean and cook, went to their own homes after each day's work. All three shared any other chores that needed to be done. A staff car and driver that was assigned to us was always at the ready. Not bad for a hoofer from Brooklyn, huh? Even though I grew up with well-to-do parents, I wasn't used to a household of servants. But believe me, you get accustomed to them very quickly. We would buy US merchandise and most foods once a week in a government building—called the NAAF. Later generations of the American military would know it as the PX, for Post Exchange. It was a grand way to live and we loved it.

We liked the food, but it took our systems time to adjust. Even though everything was washed thoroughly, after our first few meals we all broke out in a rash, which was due to the cooking we were told. And, every now and then we got what our servants called "gippy tummy"—the Egyptian version of Montezuma's revenge. We had been warned that this and other minor gastric adventures would be common, and not really dangerous unless they persisted for weeks. But, once we adjusted we really enjoyed ourselves. The servants, wearing their white gloves would serve us on our beautiful (government-supplied) china and heavy silverware. We felt like we were dining in a mansion every night, and in fact, we were. We were Honeymooners all over again.

We settled in and joined the Gezira Sporting Club, having received the necessary sponsorship from the Egyptian ministry of Foreign Affairs. The club had two swimming pools, facilities for golf and tennis, and a kids' playground. We weren't given special VIP consideration. Every American attached to the Embassy had membership to the club and similar accommodations, which became more luxurious depending on military rank. It provided a way for the all the families attached to the Embassy to stay connected. The cost to the government was virtually pennies—the standard of living being so much lower abroad. But to us it was luxury living.

So life for me was one of leisure. I didn't have to do anything except plan the day's activities, which primarily and often exclusively consisted of sightseeing, shopping and spending time with Clovis. Don was home most evenings, except when he had an overnight assignment to fly somebody somewhere in the Middle or Near East (eastern Africa). He always told me where he was going, and what he saw. But he never disclosed what the mission was about, the depth of his involvement, or any other sensitive information, which was fine by me. I knew he was a pilot, and never asked any more about it.

A typical day would find me at lunch at the club and then at the bazaars to shop. I came to like outdoor shops and still patronize them today, rather than modern department stores. Egypt was my training ground where I learned how and when to bargain. Once I became good at it, and achieved the respect of the merchants, they would often save some of the better quality items for me, once they knew what I liked to buy.

I toured all the popular spots in Cairo, or sometimes would go to the small villages in the area, usually with other officers' wives. Of these, my favorite village was called Kerdassi, about seven miles past the pyramids, which is how you measured distance in that part of Egypt. Often I would have lunch there, in a huge tent, seated on cushions. The meal was placed on a low table at just the right level for eating. By then, having adjusted to the Egyptian cuisine, I ate most everything and enjoyed it all. Lunch among the officers' wives became a big deal. You went to see and be seen, so you dressed accordingly. I loved it, because I loved to dress up and show off. The fare was exotic teas, rich-tasting cakes and cookies. In Cairo, I especially liked Groppi; the fashionable place to go for whipped creamed cake, ice cream, coffee, and tea. To make oneself presentable for these social occasions, a woman needed a beauty salon and once again Egypt was up to the challenge.

For about thirty-five cents you could have the latest style, all neatly set. I became accustomed to going every day. With all that attention to one's appearance, you'd think there had to be some place special to go after lunch. And there was, that's what the racetrack was for. There were parties too, hosted by the Ambassador, mostly at the Embassy. Everyone attached to the Embassy was invited, to mingle with an assortment of Egyptian notables. One of the frequent regulars was King Farouk, who at that time was just a skinny 26 years old kid. On his birthday they pulled out all the stops for him. Red carpets were seen everywhere, from the palace to wherever he might want to go; flags flew, bands played, and neon lights blazed all evening. There would be a party at every house where the King had a lady friend, and he had many. He frequented the American Embassy because he liked American women, and sometimes, he could be seen standing on the balcony overlooking the street, watching the beautifully dressed women pass by.

The Ambassador wasn't the only one to give parties. Most of the staff entertained to some degree, including Don and I, even though we were further down the social ladder. I had seen our servants serve as many as twelve people, with every course served perfectly and on time using small burners. It's a lesson in efficiency to watch food prepared with so few of the utensils we are accustomed to in America. It looked so easy that I thought I'd like to try my hand at cooking for guests. Naturally, I didn't start simply with a small dinner party and work up from there. Oh no, I had to have a dinner for twelve also. Announcements went out, the food was ordered and I readied myself to serve my first formal Egyptian meal. Well, what a disaster. I couldn't get the burners working properly, kerosene got all over the floor, and our disappointed dozen ended up going to a restaurant with me paying the tab. So there I was, caught up in the whirlwind of Egypt, living with Don and Clovis in very comfortable surroundings, amidst friends, without a real care in the world.

There was one custom that I found rather unsettling: thievery among the servants, which was one of the perks for them, and went on everywhere. While the servants never seemed to bother our personal belongings, things they purchased on account for the household bore close watching. I didn't say much about it, except, perhaps a general, but pointed, remark every now and then just to let them know I was aware, so it didn't get out of hand. Other than that, all things considered, it was a minor matter: the servants made life a breeze. They did everything from cook, clean, chaperone, baby-sit, make sure it wasn't too warm (Get the fans!), or too cool (Get the kerosene burners!), or whatever. When you wanted a bath the servants would scurry around with pails of water, heating them as rapidly as they could with the kerosene burners, and then pouring the warm water into the big tub. They kept pouring until it was full or you had been parboiled, or you simply said "Enough!" Clovis, who was a year and a half at the time, loved the baths. He had one every day, and he used to giggle and play with the servants waving his hands and slapping the water surface to send up sprays. He knew the servants liked to play with him too, even though they pretended otherwise. Years later, he said it was the thing he remembered most, and liked best about Egypt.

We were living a life of leisure, but I wasn't a total philistine! With so much sand and history there were many museums and sights to behold and Clovis and I saw them all. We took little side trips to Alexandria to see that old port city, and saw all the Pharaoh's tombs up and down the Nile. I even tried the camel rides out to the pyramids, and though I had reservations early on, found that I enjoyed it once I tried it. In the city, I expected to see nothing but very old buildings, maybe even tents, perhaps having seen too many Hollywood fabrications about the ancient Middle East. So in 1946 I was surprised to see many contemporary buildings. None had central heating. There was no need for it—the climate was almost always temperate. If heat was needed, we used small oil lamps when the rooms had a little morning chill. That was the extent of our climate control. That and our wardrobe, which were mostly lightweight, light-colored garments: especially shorts. The summer months were hot, very hot—you couldn't stay in the sun long at all, so everything shut down midday. Of course air conditioners hadn't been invented yet, so we didn't know what we were missing.

The shops would open again in late afternoon and remain open until dusk. That encouraged afternoon naps, an Eastern tradition. Don had to observe a military schedule and didn't get to enjoy that luxury. He had regular daily duties, and even if he wasn't flying, he was always on standby notice. As I said, he never disclosed his assignments, or the significance of them, but from time to time he would tell me about things he had seen. On one trip he flew a group of diplomats to the palace of King Ibn Saud in Saudi Arabia. He remained there for three days while the diplomats did whatever diplomats do. Don said he never saw such a place: it was—well, a palace, larger than to be believed. There were bowls of fruit everywhere, food served whenever anyone craved it, harem girls sometimes in sight and, from what he was led to believe, always available to guests. When they left, he and the diplomats were each given a gold watch and bolts of expensive silk material to make beautiful suits with. The palace, to hear Don tell it, was far grander than the King himself, who he said looked like an emaciated dirty old man.

In our little world the parties throughout the Embassy circle may not have been in a palace, but they were all elegant, glamorous affairs. With some 2,000 Americans in and around the Embassy, there was always a reason to have a party and there were always people to attend. Christmas for the Americans was a big deal. Everyone brought a gift, and no inexpensive ones were to be found. For New Year's Eve the attire was formal. The routine was a round robin; people going to one another's homes for a drink and then trekking on to the next stop. It went on all night. Our life was like a fairytale, an isolated community of privileged people. It seemed too good to last. And indeed, it didn't.

It was late evening and there was a slight chill in the air. Don was away on a mission so I was alone. The phone rang and when I said hello it was Ben calling from New York: "Is what I'm reading in the paper true?" I had no idea what he was talking about, "What are you reading?" He said there was a report of a fatal plane crash in Ethiopia and that Don's name was among the list of the dead: names and hometowns were given. I dropped the phone, and ran to the

Embassy. They said they knew nothing. I couldn't sleep all night. I tossed and turned and my mind raced with all the possibilities; maybe they are just missing, maybe Don's hurt but alive. The next morning Colonel Wyman came to my door and said bluntly, "There's been a plane crash and Don is dead." That was it. No "why" or comforting words. I was stunned, and all I could think was that a mistake had been made. "Has this been confirmed?" I asked. "There's no hope. Don is dead," the Colonel stated again, turned and walked away. Several days later Colonel McNown called and invited me to dinner. He and Don were close friends and worked together. They were like brothers; constantly in touch with each other, whether it was on the phone or in person. Don and I had dinner with he and his wife at least once a week, and I liked them very much. We talked, I cried, and he tried as best he could to comfort me. He had gone to the crash site personally and wanted to meet with me to give me Don's wedding ring. I knew then that Don was dead for sure.

For the next few days I was in shock, my heart had just been torn out. I wondered what I was to do. I was eight months pregnant with our second child and the love of my life was dead. I had been preparing a big celebration for our 3rd wedding anniversary for when he returned from his mission. But now, it began to register; he wouldn't be coming home. In a strange twist of fate the plane crashed on the exact day of our anniversary. Don was everything to me, the only man I had ever loved. The man who taught me what love was, and so effortlessly wrapped it around me.

Colonel Mcnown watched over me for many days and nights. During one day I was asked if I would go to the crash "room" and try and identify items; Don's flight jacket was there, torn to shreds. Other than the matter of fact remarks by Colonel Wyman there was no communication from the government; the officials seemed determined to be as unsympathetic as possible. Ambassador Pickney Tuck, with whom we had dined with on many occasions, never even offered his condolences to me, nor did he appear at the funeral. I felt that something was a foot, but I couldn't think straight, I was struggling just to get through the day. What would become of my son, my unborn child and me?

The government's "official" story was that Don was serving as the radio operator on a routine flight to Addis Ababa, Saudi Arabia with some foreign and American diplomats, some heavy equipment and a full crew on board. They ran into heavy rain and were flying on instruments when the plane crashed into a mountain that was 1,250 feet higher than it was listed on the map, near Dessi, Ethiopia. The plane, they said, never had a chance. There was more to the story, a lot more, which would take almost fifty years for me to learn.

It took a rescue crew thirty hours to reach the crash site on mules and horses. Colonel McNown told me it was a pretty grisly scene, so I suppose it's better I didn't see that and was left with the good memories I have now. While the rescue crew was doing it's job, the Dessi natives held traditional funeral rites for Don and the others, involving a candle light procession, chants in their language, and a circular dance around wooden boxes they built. It was a dance for the dead, I was told: that touched me. The official funeral was held later in Cairo. Some five hundred people attended, along with many diplomats stationed in that area, and even skinny King Farouk, which made Ambassador Tuck's absence all the more insulting. The Ethiopians made a huge Coptic cross and had it sent to me later after someone told them that Don had a family in Egypt. Nearly every country sent a representative to the funeral, which indicates the importance of some of the men aboard that flight. I was pleased to be able to at least go home with some memories of respectful mourners.

But, the resulting shock and stress caused by Don's death had reverberating consequences: I lost the baby. Once I recovered physically, I was ready to go home, back to New York City to put the pieces of my life together again. The Army arranged for me to be escorted and arranged to transport my personal items. It was 1947. I was on my own again, only this time with a child to support. My time with Don was over. I couldn't quite imagine what was in store for me next.

CHAPTER 14

Coasting On Empty

Clovis and I arrived to New York City alone, broke and homeless. I had truly hit bottom. I tried in vain to collect the military benefits due me from Don's life insurance, but to no avail. The government said Don's files were "missing!" What's more, all of the personal items—some of it rare and delicate items— 2,300 lbs in all; clothes, the carriage, everything, was also missing en route—as was the officer put in charge of the shipment. It would have been comical if it hadn't been so tragic. In one swift moment my entire life from Cairo—my husband, his military records, my unborn child, and all my personal belongings—vanished like a desert storm with no lingering trace.

Ben now lived in Florida and both my sisters in California. Don's family was centered in the rural Midwest, not my kind of lifestyle. I had to be someplace familiar—even if it was to be a struggle—so I stayed in New York. I wasn't completely healed from losing the baby, but Clovis and I had to eat. He was only two years old—too young to be left alone—and I knew that without a job I couldn't afford a baby sitter. It was a catch 22. And as far as finding a good, inexpensive place to live, I chose the wrong time to return to New York City. With the postwar boon starting up, apartments were impossible to find, and even if you found one, the rents were staggering. No money, no job, no prospects, no place to live, and nothing to hope for. I was desperate—Clovis and I actually slept in Central Park many nights.

I knew if I could get on solid ground, even just temporarily, to pull myself together, I would be all right. So, with nowhere else to turn, I played my last trump card—and what an Ace! I called Jimmy Durante, who happened to be staying in New York. He was pleased to hear from me and then sorry to hear what I had to say. Without hesitation, he arranged a place for me at the Astor Hotel in Times Square, one of the better-known addresses in mid-Manhattan. It was only a short-term solution, but it was enough to get me going. I couldn't ask Jimmy for anything more. He had done so much for me already over the years, and this last favor probably saved my life. I felt I should be able to take it from there. I picked up a few odd jobs and somehow managed to get a tiny room (no cooking facilities) in a cheap boarding house on West 45th Street. For days, I walked the streets with Clovis in a carriage looking for steady work, covering him when it rained. We ate our meals in the Automat on 45th Street and Sixth Avenue. I couldn't cook in the room, not even a hot plate. If I got caught at that I'd be on the street again. So it was sandwiches everyday. I wrote endless letters to the Army regarding Don and his life insurance; their sluggish response left me no resources.

I figured I couldn't go back to dancing—I had Clovis to worry about first, and second, I didn't know how well I could perform—so I asked around for other work. Eventually, I reconnected with a bartender I had known for years and he helped me get a hat-checking concession at a French restaurant, The Park Avenue, on East 52nd Street. It was owned by an ex-dancer I knew, Fanchon of the once well-known team of Fanchon and Arnold. I took the concession on consignment—$6000 a year—because I couldn't afford to buy it outright. In many restaurants and clubs a hatcheck concession, like certain other jobs such a cigarette girls (remember those young women in net stockings who could carry around a large tray filled with cigarettes, cigars, and candy, sold at ridiculous prices?) were usually not a part of the venue itself. They were sold to individuals who in turn serviced the customers in the venue. This, I thought, would tide me over until I settled on a career. My best long-term bet, I thought, was as a clothes designer, but I needed some start-up funds and some contacts before I launch anything new like that. So, till the time came, I would check hats.

Of course in addition to the fee for the exclusive rights to operate the concession, I also had to split my income with the club. It's hard to get rich doing that, especially if the owner sees you doing very well—and a pretty girl with a pretty smile can sometimes do very well. Then, they'll raise the ante, and you have no say in the matter. I was getting by, barely, because Fanchon was pretty fair with me, but I really didn't have enough money to live on. So I took a second job, checking hats at an after-hours club on 116th Street between First Avenue and Pleasant, near the FDR Drive, in Harlem. Between the two jobs, I did all right, but the hours were grueling.

The uptown club was a Mafia place run by Louie Beans, where the boys could enjoy themselves without fear of being arrested or photographed. So, they did some of the things that came natural to guys with that upbringing, and would tend to blow off a little—rather a lot—of steam from time to time. They brought beautiful women into the place, and if a girl got a little tipsy or objected to being pawed a little, they showed how tough and mean they were. I saw more women get burned with cigarettes or whacked in the face there than I had ever seen anywhere. This was new to me. Every sadist in the mob seemed to come there, and for reasons I will never completely understand, their women came with them, time and time again. And time and time again, at some time, for committing some unpredictable and petty sin, they would get abused.

These guys would carry on as if they were hosting a party in their own basement. The women were not only there as window dressing for there escorts either. In effect, the place was a bazaar. The young girls were for sale, and the other mob guys were the usual customers. If a pretty young thing attracted an important guy's attention, she could lead an almost enviable life—good food, clothes, furs, jewelry, and a free pass to all the high-class places. But, if for some reason, the girls weren't what the men expected, they'd be out the door real quick, often with a bruise or worse to show for the effort. Because many of the tough guys were ultra macho, places such as Louie Beans was a center stage for a guy looking to lean on, maim, get rid of, or acquire a girl.

And girls weren't the only commodities to be found there. In the back room was a selection of stylish fashions, including mink coats and jewelry—all of it stolen, of course. That's where those presents for the girlfriends came from. If some girl didn't like what she got, she could make nice with her boyfriend and he'd take the unwanted present into the back room and exchange it for something more to her liking. Louie Beans wasn't the only such place in the city— there were many. Fortunately for me, Louie treated me well. After I told him about my deceased husband, he was like many of the guys who escaped the draft, and had a lot of respect for the "stand-up" guys who fought in the war. Knowing about Clovis, and my need for steady work, he took a liking to me and made sure the mob guys left me alone. The money was good: I got $20 for every pack of cigarettes I sold (they cost me a dime) and $20 for checking a hat.

I was sleeping late one morning on my day off when a heard a knock at my door. When I opened it there were two guys standing there. They introduced themselves as F.B.I and asked to come in. All that I could think of was that they wanted information about Louis Beans place, and were going to lean on me to get it. "Do you know a Sergeant Christopherson Mrs. Tisdall?" they asked. "Sure I do. He was the officer assigned to arrange transport of my personal belongings from Cairo back to New York City," I said, thinking that they found my belongings. One of the guys looked directly at me asking, "Do you know where we can find him?" Are you kidding, I thought, they're asking me? "We're looking for him. He went AWOL after stealing a car," he said, and that he had four wives. They then left.

I began thinking about Louse Beans. I disliked the place. I had to get out, it was too risky, and sooner or later some violence would reach my little corner of the club. Or, the F.B.I would really show up one day looking for information. One morning at 7:00 am when I was closing the concession, without incident, I made a decision. I left by the side door and I knew I would never come back there again. Walking home I rationalized that I was now free to find something better, and I felt unafraid. But inwardly I wondered what would happen next. Whatever it was, I was starting get my spunk back, and felt I was ready for it.

Thanks to the movies, and the Sopranos, everybody today knows all about the Mafia—what they look like, what they do, how they talk or at least how they have been reinvented as entertainment. Maybe there really were (or are!) people like that, who could be polite over dinner and then take a baseball bat to a guys head over desert. Where I grew up in Brooklyn, we weren't aware of the Mafia, except for Little Augie, who was really just a neighborhood hoodlum. But the Mafia was a shadowy presence in my life, even before I realized it because they were behind many nightclubs in New York and California that I worked in or patronized. Some were pointed out to me, but I never had any dealings' with them.

When you talk about the mob and the entertainment business, two types of involvement prevailed. One was investment. The mob would put up front money to open a club or restaurant, or enlarge or finance one that was short of cash, and take a percentage of the profits. This was above board and legal, though the venue may well then have been used to launder money from less savory businesses, or the mafia may have used such illegal money to buy into the joint in the first place. If the club didn't produce profits, sometimes, they would just torch the place to collect the insurance money. The other kind of involvement was patronage, places where the mob liked to hang out, either conspicuously or low profile. The Copa is a good example. It was expertly managed with terrific food and the upper echelon Mafia people liked to visit it because their privacy would be respected. As I said, all of this formed a racy, but insubstantial background in my life, but beginning in 1947, I began to acquire a more personal knowledge of this strange subculture.

Up to this point, it probably sounds like I had a charmed life: the Aquacade, the Copa, Hollywood and Egypt—Glamour and true love. I certainly did seem to fall into wonderful things with wonderful people—up until Don was killed. But, the next few months were hell—hard times and grief compounded by military muddle and evasion. We eventually had a graveside ceremony for Don at a military cemetery in Farmingdale, Long Island. I cried when taps was played and the flag was handed to me. I'd remember this all of my life. With the military fresh on my mind I decided to follow up on the F.B.I and see how the investigation of Sergeant Christopherson was going. To my disbelief I was told that the F.B.I. had no record of two agents coming to visit me. I said, "the F.B.I. had a file, or a note, on everything, and they absolutely came to see me about Sergeant Christopherson." They then told me that the file on Sergeant Christopherson was closed—or sealed—I can't remember which. I was stunned, and frightened. Just what was going on here anyway? What was this about? It felt like I was living the plot line from a bad episode of the Twilight Zone. I didn't know what was going on but I didn't have the time or resources right now to find out. I wouldn't even know where to begin. I refocused my energy on current matters.

I needed to find a long-term apartment, and this was all that was on my mind. I remembered that Don once told me he had an old girl friend living in New York. So with nowhere else to turn I thought I'd look her up and see if she might know where I might find my own place. It was a long shot, but it was the best idea I had at the moment. Leah and Don had remained friends after they split, so she was glad to see me, and eager to hear about what happened to him. She had a small apartment at 54th Street and Lexington Avenue—midtown, a great location—where she lived with her husband Bob. I liked them both immediately, and they loved Clovis. We became friends after that first meeting, and she could see how I was living hand to mouth. But there wasn't room for us there, and Leah didn't know of any apartments. That seemed to be that. But then, another remarkable coincidence—Leah got an out-of-town job offer and decided to take it. She then suggested that I move into her place with Bob, while she tested out the new job. Bob was agreeable, since we worked on differ-ent shifts; we wouldn't get in each other's way. It seemed perfect.

After I was there a short time, Bob came into the living room one night fully dressed in women's clothing, high heels and all. From that day on he began to model his latest dresses and ensembles for me. I didn't know how to handle that or what to think, I had never encountered such a thing before, so I said nothing. I came home early one morning, after work, and found Bob and the entire ensemble from the 82 Club (a drag club) all dolled up, partying and singing, and entertaining Clovis in the process. Clovis was delighted. I was frantic. I didn't know anything about cross-dressers. What might come next? So, I decided to start taking Clovis to sleep in Central Park again. Fortunately, this bizarre state of affairs didn't last long. Leah sent word she was staying in Ohio and Bob soon left to join her there. So I had an apartment to myself at last!

I still had a problem though; the rent was too much for me to handle alone. I made contact with an old Brooklyn friend, Eleanor Fennon, who was a recent divorcee with two kids of her own. She had a job at a swanky tearoom called

Robert L. Dean's. It was a perfect setup, she worked days and I worked nights. We could watch each other's kids. By this time three months or so had passed and I had settled into my new "career," as a hatcheck girl. Another friend, Bill Empee, told me about the hatcheck concession at an uptown restaurant, the Le Vouvray on 61st Street, and I was able to get in on it, which proved very lucrative. Lots of celebrities went there as regulars, including Joyce Mathews who was in between marriages (Milton Berle going, Billy Rose coming), and, of course, lots of models. The Le Vouvray was a place for fashion models to be seen.

Our small apartment was no palace, even if I was pleased to finally have a regular home. It was a walkup in a rundown building with a rickety staircase. The paint was peeling and mice and rats scuttled in the walls. It did have a fireplace (Nice I thought) except that's where we heard the rodents scurrying about. There was no refrigerator either. You had to leave the perishables outside on the windowsill. The milk and certain other things were OK that way, but when Eleanor would leave an open can of sardines there (something she did often), every cat in the neighborhood found its way to our fire escape.

My arrangement with Eleanor worked well until she took up with a Mafia guy, Don Ferrara, who liked to punch her when she did something he didn't like. That must have happened often, because once she started dating him, she always seemed to wear some bruises or cuts, usually on her face. I'd plead with her, "What do you see in that guy? He treats you like a dog! He's going to kill you one of these times!" She'd agree, then say she loved him and that he had promised never to touch her again. Since nearly all of her boyfriends were Mafia types, no one else would go out with her now that she was "with" Ferrara. So she was trapped. If she wanted to stop doing the babysitting & work routine, her only option was Ferrara.

He eventually prevailed upon her to move into an apartment he got for her on East 36th and Madison, so he would know where she was all the time. She became a virtual prisoner, unable to have visitors unless he agreed. That left me out, because he knew I hated him. One weekend when he was out of town, a friend and I accompanied Eleanor to dinner at the Glen Island Casino in Westchester. While we were dining and listening to Glenn Miller's music, Ferrara called the apartment to check on her. When no one answered he got on a plane for New York. By the time he arrived we had long gone our separate ways and Eleanor was in bed sleeping. He woke her and beat her black and blue. When I heard about this and saw her, I told her I couldn't take it. If she was staying with him I wasn't going to see her any more. She cried, but she didn't leave him.

I learned later that she soon relied more and more on liquor to get through the day. She was always a martini drinker, and often would skip solid food to get her liquid nourishment. Even when we lived together I would come home after work and from time to time find that she had drunk more than she should have. It made me worry about Clovis and her two kids. But at that time I was on my own treadmill working two jobs, so I could only pray that she would take care of the kids while she was there with them alone. Eventually, we lost touch with one another. I heard she died of cancer. I did stay in touch with one of her kids, from time to time, as they got older. Ferrara eventually fell into disfavor with his people and ended up gay, living with his former chauffeur. Go figure.

CHAPTER 15

The Littlest Gangster

I was working at Fan and Bill's, a restaurant next door to the 21 Club on 52nd Street, when I noticed this guy who came in regularly. He always arrived at around 10:00 pm and stayed to mingle with people until long past midnight. I had a temporary assignment there, filling in at the hatcheck booth, while still working at Le Vouvray. One morning, as I was closing, he came over and said, "Hi! My name is Murray, and I've been noticing you since you started to work here. Can I invite you to breakfast?" He was all politeness and soft-spoken; he had a sort of quiet assuredness, or confidence. I told him "no," that I was busy, and promptly forgot about it.

When he found out that Eleanor was my roommate—before she was totally immersed with Ferrara—he took her to dinner one night and she invited me to join them at their table. When I did, Eleanor proceeded to tell me what a nice guy Murray was. "What's going on here?" I asked myself. At one point, perhaps by pre-arrangement, Murray got up to visit the men's room. I jumped all over Eleanor. "What are you up to?" I asked. She reached in her purse and pulled out a $200 gold Dunhill cigarette lighter. "Murray gave me this," she said, "so I would try to persuade you to go out with him." I was stunned, but also a little impressed, in spite of myself. Maybe I owed him an explanation, at least.

Eleanor left and Murray returned to a table with only me there. He bought me a drink, V.O. and ginger ale, and said thanks for joining him. I had learned previously that he was a bookie for the mob. Yet, he was easy-going and pleasant, not pushy at all, very unlike the type of guys I had seen at Louie Beans. He had a nice smile. We chatted a little, nothing memorable. Then he asked if I would go out with him. I said, "Thank you, but no, not with Clovis and the roommate situation. And quite frankly, I don't want to date a mob guy." He must have sensed I was going to be hard-nosed about this, so he didn't argue or persuade. He just nodded and said that perhaps we could have a drink together now and then. I didn't respond, but I smiled at him as he got up and left.

He didn't give up, though, and began a sort of Runyon-esque courtship. He continued to come into Fan & Bill's fairly regularly, usually shortly before closing, and would ask me again to go out and I would continually say no. Seeing how he was determined and maybe thought I was playing hard to get, I interrupted him during one of his requests; "Listen, My husband was killed in the service. I have a son to take care and I'm just scraping by, so I'm not interested in going out with anybody. I don't have time." He merely shrugged and said quietly, "I only wanted to take you to breakfast." This went on for weeks. Eventually, persistence paid off, and our first date was indeed breakfast. The topping on the cake was that it was at Reubens; where you knew you would get good food, but you never knew what the entertainment would be. Even though I had been breakfasting there off and on years earlier, I didn't realize how much I missed the place until I went back there again. People I hadn't seen in years were present, the old Copa headliners and the rest of the nightclub set.

Jerry Lewis was there; with a cap on backwards playing a frantic newsboy trying to sell newspapers, and it was like I had never left. Besides being the place for breakfast, it was also the gathering place for a series of roving party-goers. All the after-hour parties in private apartments or at various key clubs were assembled at Reubens. So here I was, back in the nightclub circuit crowd, with all the hubbub and excitement, at the center of the universe—at least at five o'clock in the morning. I had to admit that while I felt guilty about not getting home to Eleanor and Clovis right away, I did enjoy myself. We did it again some days later. Soon it was a regular date for us, a few times a week.

By that time, Murray had met Clovis and they seemed to get along. Murray indicated he would be very generous toward Clovis, given the chance. After we had been seeing each other for a while, Murray offered to give me money from time to time (a "loan" he called it—no strings attached) to help me when a lot of expenses occurred at once. I was reluctant to accept, but sometimes I did because I really needed it. I was still paying for my hatcheck concession and my job at the restaurant had no minimum salary guaranteed. In fact, nothing was guaranteed there, not even the job itself. That's because when it came to people like me—girls who worked in nightclubs or restaurants where celebrities or rich people go—we were expendable. Whatever went wrong, whenever someone important was embarrassed, it was always the fault of people in jobs like mine: hatcheck girls, cigarette girls, and the camera girls. We were scapegoats.

When I worked at the Copa years earlier I saw this first hand. We had a camera girl named Frances, a tall beautiful girl who worked hard at being popular (she later married Norman Lear, the producer of well known shows such *as*

Maude, All In The Family, Sanford & Son, Good Times, and films like *The Princess Bride* and *Fried Green Tomatoes*). The way that job worked, you got a pittance as a base salary and made commissions on pictures. Of course the more pictures she took and got print orders from customers for, the more money she made. Part of the job was getting to know the customers and having a sense of who would get a kick out of being photographed.

But, as it turned out she didn't know the clientele well enough, because there were certain people you didn't photograph. Mob guys for example. Even the FBI had trouble getting shots of them, especially the VIPs such as Albert Anastasia, who on one particular evening came into the Copa and slid into a booth next to some friends. There was a lot of hand shaking and smiling, so everybody around knew it was a happy occasion, but a very low key one. Alert for opportunities, Frances was at the banquette in an instant and began popping pictures with her big Speed Graphic. Jack Entratter saw what was happening and rushed to the banquette, which by now was drawing a lot of attention because customers were straining to see who was getting their picture taken. Jack told Frances to stop, and she thought he was just being modest or playing up to the customer, and continued shooting. Jack grabbed the camera, took all the film holders that she had already shot and exposed them to light. By this time she was too stunned and frightened to do anything except stand there with her mouth open.

Jack propelled the stunned camera girl off the floor and up the stairs to the front door, where he shoved the camera into the hatcheck booth, turned around and told the girl to get lost—you're fired. He pulled out his roll of money and gave her a few bills and told her never to come back. One of Jack's assistants had handed over her street clothes and in an instant she was out on East 60th Street, out of a job, and still wondering what had happened. The whole episode, which I witnessed, took only a few minutes.

When I thought about getting more involved with Murray, this is the kind of thing I remembered. I wondered if he had this same need for privacy? Could he go from all smiles to a tirade in a passing moment? I really didn't know anything about his "career" in the mob, but early on, he told me (or rather "asked," though I knew I didn't have any choice in the matter) never to ask or talk about his business, his clients, his territory (the lucrative upper East Side), or his business routine. "Never ask me about my business," would become a cliché in many mob movies in years to come, including the Godfather. But those were the actual words he used. Murray was not a talkative person as a rule, but he wasn't the Sphinx either. He could tell a good story, but he rarely talked about his mob friends or what they did. And from what I had seen and heard about the Mafia, I didn't want to know, or be any closer to them.

Still they were there in the background. In the first few weeks of our almost-daily meetings for breakfast, I wondered if I was being checked out because I was an outsider spending time with one of their men. Murray told me that girls were OK, as far as his bosses were concerned, because all guys should have a girl or two. But they had to be the right type; not too smart, not too greedy, and not too inquisitive. Many of the mob-connected "girlfriends" I met actually were smart, but played dumb to stay in one piece. If they toed the line, they would have a luxury apartment, gorgeous clothes, meals and drinks at the best places, and exotic vacations. The only risk, besides getting too inquisitive, was getting too old. Mob guys liked their girls young and sexy, and smart enough to know their place. I knew right away how to adapt. Having worked for some egomaniacs (Billy Rose comes to mind, as do some of the Hollywood bozos I ran into), I knew how to play the game.

When Eleanor moved out of our place to be with Ferrara, I was suddenly responsible for the entire rent myself. This would have been very difficult for me, so when Murray suggested I move in with him,—just temporarily, I agreed. Any qualms I had about Murray were put aside because he seemed so Low-key, and for a mob-guy, frankly, he was fun to be with. Clovis seemed to like him too. His place on 33rd Street and Third Ave. was small, being a studio apartment, but it was pleasant. And a previous tenant had painted lush land-scape murals on the walls that Clovis and I relished. One morning as we were finishing breakfast at Reubens, I got ready to go home to Clovis who was with a baby sitter at the apartment, when Murray asked me to linger a minute, he had something to suggest. I thought it was another show he had tickets for, or, even worse, another mob "testimonial" I had to accompany him to. (How I hated those intra-family social affairs!) So I waited, cautiously. But he sur-prised me. He told me he knew of an apartment building at East 55th Street at 1st Avenue where he could get a larger apartment. He wanted me to move in with him, permanently. There would be plenty of room, even a bedroom for Clovis. He'd pay for everything: rent, utilities, food, even clothing for Clovis and me. I was stunned. I didn't expect this. The pragmatic side of me said: "Don't do anything rash!" I paused, "Let me think about it, Murray."

I did think about it. Moving in with Murray meant no more hatcheck work, no more all-night jobs, no more worrying about Clovis, no more cheap food and cheap clothes, essentially, no more poverty. What would be the downside? Having Murray as a boyfriend? Murray hadn't even made a serious pass at me. I knew he was greatly attracted to me, but he had never tried to force me into bed with him. Besides, I liked the guy. He was attentive, humorous, generous, and sweet—not like so many of those mob guys that knocked their girlfriends around. I was fussy, and so was Murray in his way. We both liked nice things.

We both enjoyed going out, rather than staying home nights. He seemed to be as fond of Clovis as any father would be. So, using my best judgment, I decided to say "yes."

Murray didn't say much when I told him the next evening, but that was like him. He knew I'd weigh the pros and cons, see the benefits, and say "yes." To his credit, he didn't push, didn't try to oversell the idea. He got me. But, getting the apartment wouldn't be as easy. There would be a few months wait and, once I saw it I realized it was too small. Murray may not have thought so right away, but he came round to my point of view when I pointed out (1) I had a lot of clothes and would get more. (2) Clovis had a lot of clothes and toys and other stuff, he would get more, and (3) he, Murray, had a lot of clothes and would get lots more, the way he purchased wearing apparel, not to mention gadgets, appliances, food and whatever. He knew where I was headed, and so he took the building manager aside and had a long talk, during which, I can guess, some money exchanged hands. We ended up with a bigger apartment on the 13th floor, facing north. I liked the apartment and the neighborhood; it was quiet, had good restaurants, and was close to subways and buses.

The apartment had two bedrooms, one of which I made into something nice for Clovis; a living room, a small kitchen—into which I managed to cram a small table and chairs—lots of closets, and a foyer large enough for a small dinning table and four chairs. The building had mahogany-paneled elevators, a round-the-clock doorman, and lots of heat. This was before air conditioning, which was put in later. In short, it was a luxury building. Living there enabled me to see the side of Murray I had missed. I knew he liked clothes, but I never realized how much he liked them. His taste was expensive. He had his suits and jackets made to order. He owned dozens and dozens of shirts, socks, accessories, throwing out or giving away the old ones as he brought in the new. His specialty was neckties—he had what seemed to be hundreds of them; he'd buy expensive silk ones by the dozen.

He also liked expensive gadgets, such as "time-saving" kitchen devices of all kinds even though he didn't know how anything worked in the kitchen. In those days a TV set was high-tech, and we had one of the first. He also refurnished compulsively. Just as he couldn't resist a new gadget, he couldn't stand a certain décor for long. He'd be lying in bed, watching TV or reading, and he'd suddenly say, "I can't stand the color of that wallpaper any more," and the next day the place would be filled with decorators, painters, plasterers, electricians, whoever and whatever, with their wallpaper samples, paint sample chips, new fabrics, and new rug samples. Murray redecorated at the slightest whim. He wouldn't care how short a time period had passed since the last redecoration. He'd do one room at a time, or a few rooms, and sometimes, it'd be the whole apartment, or just as likely, just one wall. I never knew what to expect. These decisions seemed to come upon him suddenly, spontaneously. If he could have gotten wallpaper hangers in the middle of the night, he'd have done it. That's the way he was.

It didn't bother me. I learned to stay away during these periods. There was a certain amount of frenzy to these alterations, because Murray was always in a hurry. Since he paid everybody in cash, all these craftsmen and artisans broke their necks to get things done promptly. In the time we lived there, we went through French provincial, Italian, Spanish, modern; you name it, we had it. And of course each style change meant new rugs, furniture and accessories. His spending didn't end with the apartment and he always bought me new clothes, because he wanted me to look good too. He paid cash for everything, so I never knew how much anything was; there was never a bill.

But his special pleasure was buying clothes for Clovis. In addition to the usual infant boy and pre-school stuff, he'd buy miniature adult clothes, such as three-piece suits with hats, shirts and neckties. Soon Clovis looked like a miniature version of Murray—that is, dark blue pinstripes, designer shirts and ties, black wingtip shoes, dark fedora hats, a gold bracelet—diamond and ruby pinky rings—and initials on the cuffs of his shirts. At one point, Clovis complained, "I look just like the Untouchables! People think I'm a "midget gangster!" And, Murray didn't just dress Clovis like one of the boys he treated him that way. For a five-year old child Clovis had a pretty exotic social life, because Murray would sometimes take Clovis with him on his nightly rounds, perch him up in a banquette at the *Stork Club* or *21*, and do his thing while Clovis sat there and watched the people looking at him as they strolled by. He would get fed and kissed and hugged (in a nice way) by all kinds of famous people, and quickly became used to the attention. One of his early baby sitters was Barbara Walters, who more than a few times watched over him as a favor to Murray, at the Latin Quarter, which was managed by her father, Lou.

Clovis was always so bright as a little boy, so much more adult than other kids his age, but I knew his day/night routine wasn't right, if not for his education, certainly not for his health. He needed some routine, some discipline, not with adults who would be fawning over him like a little movie star all the time. My first attempt to get him into a structured environment was letting him stay with my mother's sister in Huntington, Long Island, about an hour away, and going to see him every weekend. Eventually, I saw that the arrangement wasn't working. Clovis was depressed there, and my aunt was getting peeved about having an active child around.

Next, I enrolled him in a boarding school: the New York Military Academy, in Cornwall-on-the-Hudson. Technically he was too young to attend, but they allowed him to live on campus because Don died in the service. Each day he was driven into town to the elementary school. Looking back now, I realize I missed having Clovis around all of the time in those years, but it pleased me to know that Don's military service afforded Clovis a good education. (Don's army pension finally came through after a chance encounter with a general in retirement!) Moreover, Clovis did well in school and he seemed to like it. When he was nine, Don's sister, Pearl, and her husband Colonel Ted Stanford-Blunden offered to let Clovis go with them to Germany for three years, where Ted was stationed. It sounded like a good experience, so I let him go.

Clovis

Murray was a gentleman by instinct and never made a scene, even though he must have had some bettors skip out on their bets, or plead here and there for a few more days to pay off. Still, he never had any difficulties running his book. He really liked people and they sensed it, even though he wasn't a back-slapper or glad-hinder. He rarely raised his voice nor was he demonstrative. To watch him do his thing from a distance was to see a guy talking what looked to be small talk, to a steady stream of people. He'd sit in one place, usually nursing a club soda, until his business was concluded, then he'd move on to the next stop. At some places, he'd only stay a few minutes while at others he'd be there for a while, whatever it took. He had a quick mind, especially with numbers. He could add a column of figures in a flash. I never saw him pay off anybody, although I did see a lot of people give him gifts, quietly. He was well liked by club owners and headwaiters, many of which, were customers. His day would start about 10 pm and he would be out until after the clubs closed at 4 am. Then I'd usually meet him somewhere, maybe Reubens for breakfast or the Gold Key Club. Sometimes, with a bartender in tow, we'd end the evening by going to Mulberry Street for Italian food.

So, that was our social routine—amiable rituals that I settled into easily enough. Private life was another matter. When Murray and I set up housekeeping together I didn't know what to expect in the way of sex. I had told him all about my marriages and romances; he had told me he had never married, but I presumed, correctly, he had slept with many girls. So I was ready for most anything, except what really happened: nothing! We shared a bed but he got in it and went immediately to sleep. I didn't say or ask anything, I felt it was up to him to make the first move. Finally, he did, but it was no love scene. He was only interested in himself, not in sharing pleasure. When he was done, he pushed me away and turned back to his own side of the bed. "Well", I thought,

"Ok, if that's the way he wants it." I knew then I could never love Murray, because he didn't know how to love. I figured he was accustomed to hookers or cheap one-night stands, because that's how men are when they just need a woman for sex: cold and unfeeling.

CHAPTER 16

Central Park On The Rocks

In the eight years we were together, Murray and I only had sex three times, and each time it was the same as the first: detached, quick, and unfeeling. I merely endured it. I never criticized or asked questions or said anything. I think he knew what I was thinking. But, this lack of love didn't change our relationship, it just defined it a little better—we were a good working friendship, not a love match. Because of the almost platonic nature of our life then, I was able with a clear conscience to have my own little discreet flings when I wanted to—not often, but enough times to make me feel like a woman.

One of those flings occurred on a bright summer day at the height of the summer. My friend and I took a walk to Central Park and we stumbled across a huge rock. We sat and kicked off our shoes. After talking and many kisses and hugs we started to make love. When I opened my eyes, I said, "Smokey don't move, we are near a bridge and there are at least ten people looking down at us. When I count to three get up and run." We did, and everyone started to clap and cheer. OK, so not every fling was discreet. We laughed about this adventure many times and remained friends for many years. And though we tried, we never could find the same spot by the rock.

I was always able to rationalize my life style, to convince myself that what I had—a generous benefactor who really asked little of me, except to be there with him when he wanted me, was what any girl would want. I cared for Murray, even if I could never love him. He was kind and generous to me and to Clovis, and came into my life at a time when I needed somebody. And despite the sexual coldness between us, we became like a family. Most Fridays, he'd take Clovis and me to his parent's house, where we had dinner. The house was not an elegant one, a really no-frills living place with minimal furniture; not well kept. Murray's mother was a sweet, small, fat woman with a nice smile and easy disposition. His father on the other hand was selfish and peevish: I didn't like him at all. So it was with some satisfaction that I ignored him and tried instead to make Murray's mother a little happier with attention and gifts. Murray never tried to interfere, so he must have felt the same way about his father as I did, even if he never said so. I came to realize that I was more considerate to Murray's family than he was. He disliked going there. I could see that, and, I guessed that it was because he didn't want to be reminded of his humble roots. He rarely talked about his childhood, but I did discover that he left home when he was only twelve years old, lived with mob guys in his neighborhood, and started running numbers for them. But, other than this uncomfortable relationship with his parents, Murray was the most generous person I ever met, verging on being a spendthrift. I thought I was a great buyer! Murray was far out of my class when it came to spending money.

For instance, tipping. In our nightly rounds of trendy spots like 21, the Palm, or the Copa, Murray never tipped less than $50. That seemed to be his minimum, so no wonder they all knew and loved him! He wasn't just a big tipper in public places like nightclubs or restaurants, he tipped equally well to the doormen and elevator operators in our building, and a workman doing a job in our apartment would always get a magnanimous tip; if he did the job reasonable well. I asked him once how much he had to spend each night doing his job, and I suggested maybe $1000 or $2000 a night. He said, "Yeah, I guess that's about right." He didn't boast about it or believe that it made him special. It was just the way he was. Christmas gave him a chance to overspend on everybody, and he did. We always had a huge tree, with mounds of presents spilling out from under it. To buy for him however, was difficult. He had nearly everything, so if you gave him something for Christmas (I guess, working for the mob, you had to celebrate Christmas, Jewish or not) that he didn't like or want, he'd turn around immediately and give it to the doorman or somebody like that.

As a bookmaker Murray never sampled his own wares—horses. But, he knew where all the crap games in town were—in a sewer, or on a boat, in an empty building, wherever, he knew and he followed them. He loved to gamble, but only dice and cards. My first-hand knowledge of his gambling came from the weekend sessions he'd set up at our apartment. For a while, it seemed as if every weekend he'd arrange for a marathon poker and craps session with his Mafia friends. They would come individually into the apartment, sometimes four, sometimes six or more, and play from Friday night until Monday morning, when they would settle accounts, count their money, get dressed (they'd be in T-shirts by the time Sunday rolled around), clean up the dirty dishes, take out the garbage, and then give me my apartment back

The first few times Murray arranged his poker game, I ignored his suggestion to go out somewhere and I stayed around to watch. Finally, I got bored. I trained Murray to tell me early on when he had scheduled a game so I could take Clovis on a weekend with friends or even stay over at a neighbor's. This was the only imposition Murray ever made on our domestic life—I didn't resent it. He never told me whether he was a winner or not, even though I used to ask. All he'd say was, "I did OK." They played for big money; thousands of dollars were on the table at any given time. But I think it was the excitement, trying to bluff each other, and the laughs that they played for and enjoyed— after all, they all had plenty of dough. If this was a vice, it was the only one Murray had. He believed money was there to spend. Maybe because he didn't have to worry much about where it came from or how long the flow would last. He never saved a dime that I was aware of.

Murray was popular with his "work associates," and had obligatory social engagements, such as weddings, and anniversaries, usually involving a family member of the higher-ups. Sometimes I'd go with him, but I preferred not to. I was never comfortable at those affairs, and neither was he. Not that he was anti-social—we ate out every night. He was pretty understanding about my discomfort, and sometimes, when there was a poker game or some other mob thing Murray had to deal with, he'd send me to Miami Beach, Florida, "just to give me a change of scenery." He sometimes didn't even need a reason.

You might think that such a lifestyle would get boring after a while. Well, to be honest, it doesn't. If anything, it was always new and exciting because so many different things kept happening. The more I got to know Murray, the more I could share his humor, and we'd laugh when someone was chewing loudly and he'd say, "What's the name of that tune?"

Murray wasn't flamboyant. You'd overlook him in a crowd. In spite of his work and the people he hung around with, he was never arrested or accused of anything illegal. Murray was careful. I never knew how or when he met with the mob people and I never saw him go into a bank or cash a check. If Murray had a value system, it was based on material things of good quality. Better to have one excellent suit rather than one half-dozen cheap ones he'd say. Murray's clothes were not only expensive they were kept in fastidious condition. Everything was neatly pressed, especially the pants, which had to have a razor-sharp crease to satisfy him. I was prompted to use that fetish as a way of getting Murray to keep his promises.

We'd occasionally have dinner parties, mostly with Murray's friends, and it would be up to me to play hostess. I didn't have to cook, it would be a catered meal, or, we'd just have drinks. But, after being made to feel awkward a few times, because Murray would show up later, I told him that the next time he was late for these occasions I'd cut his favorite pair of pants in half. He laughed. Sure enough though, the next time he was late, I went into his closet, found a new, expensive pair of woolen slacks and cut them off at the knees, then left them outside the door in the hallway. When Murray came home, he walked in carrying the pieces of his pants. After that, he got home on time for dinner parties.

Everything in life has a cycle, and so too my life with Murray had to end sometime. Eventually I wanted out, not because I was bored, or didn't have enough, or wanted to be with someone else. Clovis was still in Germany and it dawned on me that after eight years I was in the same spot as when Murray found me working as a hatcheck girl. I was going nowhere and getting older doing it. I had no security. I had nothing in the bank and nothing to look forward to. Murray's concern was only with the here and now, with material things. I wanted something more. I knew what I wanted and that it wasn't what I had now. So, I politely asked him to leave. After trying to dissuade me, he agreed we would try a trial separation, and he moved into the Dover Hotel at 56th and Lexington.

He had only been gone about a week when Lynn called somewhat excited, "Harriet, I need to move out tonight", she said. "I can't be with Frankie anymore, and if I'm here when he gets home he'll talk me into staying." I was getting ready to go out for the evening, so I told her, "Bring your things and come stay with me for a while, I'll leave the key under the mat for you." Lynn was a dancer and we had been friends for years. A tall blonde knockout, she turned the head of any man who saw her, and she was never at a loss for male suitors if she wanted them.

When I walked through the door later that night I was shocked. My living room looked like a second hand furniture store. What I didn't realize was that when I said bring everything and stay here for a while, that she was going to bring "everything" and stay for over a year. I helped her unpack, and then on the spur of the moment I suggested, "Let's take a trip to Florida for a week!" It would give me a chance to relax and rethink the direction of my life, as well as my relationship with Murray. Lynn too, I imagined, needed to sort out her own mind. We really didn't think about it. We just threw some clothes in a bag, and with $400.00 each and Frankie's car we were off—some 50 years before Thelma and Louise made it fashionable.

We arrived at the outskirts of North Miami and pulled into a little hotel. The room was smelly and musty and I couldn't stay there another night. We decided to take a short weekend trip. I was nervous on this little 10-seat island hopper, so I stayed focused on Havana. This was pre-Castro Cuba, when Americans were welcome, and this would be only the first of many trips I would make there. We went immediately to Hotel National for lunch, the #1 hotel on the island. If you want to meet good people you have to go to good places I always say. We went to the bar and ordered two cold drinks while we read the menu. The bartender returned with the drinks, informing us that they were compliments of Mr. Jose Ferre. Lynn began to look around but I quickly kicked her. "Don't look around, he obviously saw us and when he's ready he'll introduce himself," I said. In the meantime we ordered some steak sandwiches and ate our lunch.

About an hour later a thin well dressed man, about 5'9" approached us. "Hello ladies, my name is Jose Ferre," He was very charming and couldn't take his eyes of Lynn. We chatted small talk for a little while, and then he asked us if we would like to join him on his yacht for the next week as he toured the Caribbean islands. Lynn was about to speak but I cut in, "We can't travel with you on your yacht. We don't even know you, what if we have a fight? How do we get back?" Lynn was visibly disappointed. He said he'd like to get to know us and asked if we would like to be his guests for the grand opening of a new hotel in Veradero Beach, Cuba the next day. We accepted.

Morning came quickly, we rose late, and barely got ready in time to meet the chauffeured car Jose sent for us. The affair began in the afternoon, so people were dressed casual yet elegant, much like you would expect at a polo match or an afternoon party in the Hampton's (an exclusive beach resort in Long Island, NY). It was a splashy grand affair. Latin bands set the mood. There was a pig roast, and Champagne, lots of Champagne. Against the beautiful tropical landscape, TV cameras and reporters roamed the party like hunters on the prowl for "celebrity meat."

We soon came to realize that our host was a wealthy, influential and politically connected industrialist known as the "cement king of Ponce" (Ponce is in Puerto Rico), one of the wealthiest men in the Caribbean. As the cameras flashed all around us Lynn and I flashed our big smiles, which wasn't just for show—we were having a grand time. But for two young girls who had just left their spouses—mob spouses—one with abrupt notice and the other without any, being on TV may not have been the smartest thing we could have done. But we got swept up in moment and the tropical mood, so caution was thrown to the wind, and we didn't give New York City a second thought.

Our weekend quickly turned into a week as we traveled with Jose from island to island throughout the Caribbean, a round trip airplane ticket always in hand. Jose and Lynn were inseparable, which may have just been the excitement of the moment, but I suspected that they were falling for each other. I don't know if it was Jose's good nature, guilt, or the path of least resistance when he insisted that I go anywhere I want, do whatever I want, buy whatever

I want and charge it all to him. I went pencil happy! Lynn came back to the room one morning and stopped dead in her tracks. "Harriet, where did all this stuff come from?" I grinned, and told her, "While you're out screwing around, I've been out shopping around."

On an island stop to Santa Domingo we met President Trujillo one night while his son-in-law taught me the "*Meringue*," a popular dance in the islands, which later found it's way to America. It didn't really register with us how dangerous it was to be there. But Jose's words echoed in my head years later when I learned of the iron-fisted dictatorship that Rafeal Trujillo ruled over. "Stay close to me," Jose said, "because if you wander off on your own and they want to keep you, there is nothing I can do—I would have to let you go." As Americans we just have difficulty really taking any of that kind of talk seriously. Lynn and I were lucky that we heeded his wishes and stayed close. The things I would see later in my life persuaded me that in fact those things do happen.

Every night with Jose was a party, even if it was just four of us having dinner. He was charming, delightful and seemed to be a genuinely nice person that indulged his friends; everything had to be the best! He even tried to play matchmaker for me, always inviting a date to accompany me to dinner. But, the only men he seemed to know were those of royalty; the banana king, the sugar king, the pineapple king—you get the idea. One night during yet another blind date I leaned over and said, "Listen Jose, I don't like these guys. When I find someone I like I'll let you know." Meanwhile the coffee king had just offered to take me to Paris. "I don't have the clothes," I said, and he quickly offered to buy them for me when we got there. But what's the point of going to Paris with some guy I didn't like.

I went to the lobby to get my messages from the hotel in Florida, and to return a call to Sol and Sunny, two 7th Ave fashion manufacturers whom Lynn and I were supposed to meet in Miami the week before. It seemed that we were engaged in a never-ending game of phone tag with them leaving messages, and us doing the same—and it was now our turn. It was a reality check when I realized we had now been traveling with Jose for over two weeks, with no end in sight.

As I turned to return to the dining room I almost ran over this tall man in a white uniform. He was gorgeous, striking really. "Hello, my name is Bruce Johnson," he said. "I was quite taken with you in the dinning room. I hope I didn't misunderstand your intentions, but when I heard you turn down that trip to Paris, I got the feeling you were not really interested in that fellow. So, I came out here in the hopes of meeting you." Maybe it was the heat, the sun, or the drinks—but I was star struck. "Are you alone," I asked, "your such a doll?"

When he told me he was I said, "Don't move, I'll be right back!" I rushed back into the dinning room, grabbed Jose and said, "I found him," and ushered him to the lobby where Bruce was curiously waiting. Jose graciously invited Bruce to join us for the weekend, and Bruce accepted, but only if he could pay his own way.

He was a Navy geologist, stationed in Havana. Tall, blonde and blue eyed, Bruce made me giddy with delight. So with my new heartthrob in tow, we were off to the next stop on our Caribbean-wide tour. My shopping sprees were fun, but would now come back to bite me in the...ear. Having had my ears recently pierced on one of those shopping expeditions, one of them had become infected. I wanted to spend the night with Bruce, but the pain was too unbearable, so it wasn't going to happen. Maybe he would be one of those "the one who got away" stories I thought. But I did see him again, back in New York, several months later. Somehow the glow had faded. Maybe it was the magic of an accidental romance, a balmy night in a tropical paradise, or perhaps just the uniform. I don't know what it was, but even with his still dashing good looks, the spark was gone.

Lynn and Jose continued to occupy each other's time. We had been traveling now for five weeks. We toured every island, met fascinating people, went to lavish parties and dinners, saw fabulous shows and danced the night away. It wasn't what we had planned when we left New York City with our $400, but we weren't complaining. But it was now time for us to go back to Miami. True to form Jose gave us plane fare to fly back to New York City, not knowing that we had a car waiting for us back at our Florida hotel. So we did the only thing that any young girls in our situation could do. We cashed in the tickets, picked up our clothes from the musty hotel and promptly checked into the Fountain Bleau Hotel on Collins Ave., the finest accommodations along the famous Miami Beach strip.

After a five week whirlwind adventure, Lynn was having a sudden panic attack, worried about the wrath of Frankie that faced her back in New York City. "Look, the guys are going to be just as upset whether we're gone five weeks or six," I told her. "Let's just enjoy our last week and deal with them when the time comes." We had been at the Fountain Bleau all week when Sunny and Sol showed up to spend the weekend. The next few days we partied around the clock, dancing, dinning and seeing shows. I didn't really like Sunny, but we were all having a good time together, even though I thought he was a bit cheap. Then again, maybe that's not fair. After all, who could possibly have followed in Jose's shoes? By the end of the weekend Lynn and I were exhausted, and needed a vacation from vacationing. We were ready to go home.

The engine in our Pontiac was idling, while Lynn talked to Sol through the rolled down window. Being playful, not really expecting much, she asked him for some gas money. "$100," he protested, "I could go to dinner with Lana Turner for that kind of money." It wasn't so much the money as it was the principle I think. She shot back, "Then go find Lana Turner you cheap skate." An argument erupted and Sol countered that he was not a cheap skate, as though saying it loud made it so. As they continued to argue he began to throw money into the car through the open window as if to prove a point. While they were verbally jousting I began to count. $50, $100, $200, $300…"what," Lynn said, only partly listening to me. "$300, let's go, go, go," I insisted. She stomped on the gas and we were off. It took a while for the whole experience to set in. We left New York City with $400 each, to go to Florida for a week at a cheap hotel. We ended up spending five weeks seeing the best of the Caribbean, in the most lavish of style, an additional week at Miami Beach's best resort hotel, and were returning home with more money than we left with—life can be such an adventure when you just let it happen.

Meanwhile, our men, Murray and Frankie were anxiously waiting for us as we arrived; peeking out of the bedroom window as we drove up. If Frankie was unsure as to why he returned home to an empty apartment five weeks earlier, he must have had a hint by now after seeing all of Lynn's belongings in my apartment. I had called Murray when we were leaving Florida to let him know that we we're OK and on our way home. Neither of them was angry with us, Frankie was so love with Lynn he couldn't have been angry with her. From that day forward, even after she got remarried, Frankie would check in on her from time to time to make sure she was all right, inquire as to whether she needed any money, and to this day, now in their 80s, he still does.

Murray assumed I was on some kind of trip, as I had taken several during our relationship. What he didn't know was that I had come to a decision. I told him the next morning that I didn't want him to come back. (Some nerve, huh? He found this place and moved us into it, and now, I was giving him the heave-ho.) It was difficult because I cared about Murray. He was always there for me, materially. But, I wanted, and needed, a lover, a friend, someone to build a life with. And Murray wasn't a life companion; he was a benefactor and good time buddy. I wasn't hinting marriage; I knew he didn't want that because he had said so years earlier, and I didn't want it either, not with him. He tried to interrupt me, saying he'd get a big house in California with a big swimming pool, thinking that would be the kind of security that would satisfy me. I told him these were only material things. And California? Talk about shooting a hole in the boat! He realized, at least in concept, what I was saying. Though I don't think he ever really understood the substance of it—he saw life differently than I did.

Having made a pretty good attempt to dissuade me, he finally said, "OK," and returned to the Dover Hotel. We lost touch, except for a couple of colorful incidents, typical of our whole relationship. A week or so after he had left, I was hosting a party of ten to twelve friends, and we were all a little tipsy and playing a game called Sniff and Strip. It called for male and female partners to pass on an orange to one another without their hands; the orange would be placed under one chin, and then passed to the partner's chin. Whoever dropped the orange had to take off an item of clothing. (If you've seen the Cary Grant, Audrey Hepburn movie Charade—this is the game they're playing in the nightclub scene—talk about "meet cute"!)

The game was just getting interesting when I heard the doorbell. It was Murray, saying he was going to sleep there tonight. I told him "no, I'm having a party!" I was truly angry. There were couples everywhere in various stages of nudity. But he came inside anyway, took off his shoes, and fell asleep on the couch. One by one the couples left, I went to bed, and the next morning Murray was still there. When he left it would be the last time I saw him in New York. He did call one more time, obviously at a crap game and wanted to know if I had $2500 in cash. I told him, truthfully, that I didn't. Weeks later I heard rumors that Murray had left town. He owed an $18,000 debt he couldn't pay off. And in a few months, Murray was a memory.

I felt sad, but deep down I knew I had done the right thing. I was living on my own again. A year later I got phone call late at night. It was Murray. He was in Chicago and had a job as the manager of the Playboy Club, a new thing started by the magazine publisher, Hugh Hefner. I was glad to hear he was OK and doing well. A few months later he called again to invite me for a weekend visit. On the 4th of July, I was wined and dined by Murray and his two friends, Howie and Marge Wong. We ate, drank, and had a lot of laughs. I saw the Playboy bunnies and the city sights. Hugh Hefner was a very low key charming man, and we enjoyed a day on his magnificent yacht. Of course there were Playboy bunnies everywhere, though they seemed to me the unhappiest little vixens I had ever met.

Murray was the same as ever—new clothes, new gadgets, and new jewelry as a present for me. It was wonderful. Just before I left on Sunday, he asked me to stay on, to live with him again. There was lots of room he explained: it wouldn't cost me a cent. Clovis could come too, and so on. I had to refuse. It would have evolved into the same relationship, with the same limitations as before. So I returned to New York, happier for the trip and now the proud owner of a new mink coat, a gold bracelet, and a pair of Chihuahua puppies named Bambi and Gambi.

Murray and I remained friends for 40 years. We had talked about another visit to Chicago, but when he called to invite me, I got so excited that I tripped over a pair of shoes I had left on the bedroom floor, and broke my back. I wasn't able to go, needless to say. He sent me money for airfare in 1985 for another visit, but that was two days before he had the stroke and died.

CHAPTER 17

Weekend In The Jug

It was the mid-1950s, Murray was gone, and I was embarking on a new life, again. It had less security but also more open possibilities to fill whatever void still existed in my life. The next few years flew by. While living in Stuttgart, Germany with Don's sister pearl and her husband, Clovis lived in grand style. He even studied fashion at The Sorbonne, a famous school in Paris. It was a great experience for a boy of eleven. However, while he and Ted enjoyed each other's company, Pearl would punish him often for hanging around with the kids of the enlisted men, rather than officers' families. Pearl was too rank conscious, I guess, or maybe just a snob. She was also a lush, as it turns out, well into her martinis early in the day. So after three years, I made arrangements to bring him home. Still, despite punishing him regularly, Pearl adored Clovis and didn't want him to leave. She threatened that if I attempted to bring him back to the United States, that she would fight me in court; showing that I was a bad mother—I lived a "sorted life," according to her—and have Clovis taken away from me. A quick reminder of her behavior aboard a cruise from Alaska, and she quickly forgot the entire affair.

I got a new hatcheck concession at the Madison Mayflower, on Madison and 69th Street, a sophisticated private dining and drinking restaurant that also featured very high ladies of the evening. The money was very good. But, just when I thought I might be getting back on solid ground, I was reminded how quickly things can change. On Thursday night before Memorial Day weekend of 1962, at our busiest hour, I heard a lot of commotion and shouting around the front door. It soon moved into the bar area. I could see policemen herding everybody together—customers, waiters, bartenders, the ladies, the madams, even the owner, where they could make sure no one got away. Then they took names and marched everybody outside, where police wagons were waiting.

The raid didn't just include the madam, the boss, the girls and their customers, but every one of us: the cook, the bartender, and, of course, me—the hatcheck girl. Out we went into the street and into police wagons. The men were taken in one direction and we in another: the women's jail at Sheridan Square in Greenwich Village to be exact. It was almost funny. I'd lived for almost eight years with a minor mobster, without any trouble, and now, I was in the slammer. What a pigsty! From the outside, it looked like a quaint miniature castle, with red brick walls and a rounded turret on top: a colorful, bright spot on the city landscape. But inside it was dirty, crowded and noisy. We were booked and fingerprinted and put by pairs into cells to await our court appearance. After we had been jailed for an hour or so, we learned that due to the long holiday weekend we would be there until the next possible court appearance, Monday morning, four days away!

All I could think of was that someone at the restaurant forgot a payoff, and this was punishment. You could be sure everyone from the mayor to the cop on the beat knew about this place. Moreover, we knew that someone downtown in the DA's office or the police department was a special boyfriend of the madam, who usually tipped the club off about raids. "Get the girls out," he'd call and tell his madam girlfriend, "The boys will be dropping in tonight." On this occasion however, I heard later—after all the girls, including the madam, were solidly behind bars—that somebody called downtown and asked if the madam should be locked up also. "She can rot there," came the answer. So much for love!

So there we were, twelve women, including all the ladies of the evening, locked up. Those four days were long and loud. The girls were yelling out the windows at their men friends below in the street or were screaming for attention from the few guards on duty, who ignored everything and everybody. We got slop for meals. I was afraid to eat any of it, except the crusts from the bread. The coffee had some stuff in it I didn't recognize, so I drank nothing except a taste of water now and then. After being there a few hours, my head ached constantly. Our bedding was a paper-thin, dirt-encrusted piece of cloth for a blanket. No pillow, no mattress, only a spring. Our nearest neighbors were some black girls without any teeth, but that didn't prevent them from yelling at us continually. Things quieted down a bit during the night, but not much. Then we could hear the rats eating the newspapers. My cellmate was a tall blonde who looked more like a showgirl than a call girl. She was quiet, resigned. She had been through this before.

We got our traditional one phone call. I used mine to call a neighbor to look in on Clovis, to make sure he got fed and taken care of while I was gone. On Monday they hauled all of us downtown for our court appearance. The club owners sent a lawyer to meet us, who told us to say nothing except "yes" or "no" or "I don't know I just worked there." Great advise, which ended up costing me $1500. The hookers were charged with prostitution and got 30-day sentences. I was charged with "vagrancy" and given a suspended sentence. I was told to go home, forget the whole business, and consider myself lucky. Being in debt for $1500 and now out of a job I really didn't feel especially lucky. But I was glad to be out of that brick prison.

I received a call from the owner of the Mayflower a few days later telling me his place was open again, and I should come back to work. I told him to forget it. The thought of another visit to the women's detention center in Sheridan Square scared the hell out of me. I didn't want to seek out any more trouble, or even the potential for trouble. Of course that didn't stop trouble from finding me. Several days later two detectives flashed their badges to the doorman, asked what apartment I was in, and then went directly to the elevator. They sat in my kitchen and came on like big brothers. They knew about my arrest and they were there to "help" me get back my hatcheck concessionaire license back, they said. All it would cost me was $1500. In short, it was a shakedown. Looking one and then the other straight in the eye, I told them that the restaurant was raided, that I hadn't been charged with anything except vagrancy, and that my license was still in force. But they were determined. After a lengthy debate I finally threw them out.

But they didn't forget about me. I began getting phone calls at all hours reminding how much it would cost me to work again. Whenever I went outside the building they'd be sitting there in a car waiting for me. "Hello, Harriet, how's business?" They'd proceed to follow me down the street until I would go in a different direction against traffic to lose them. I finally got so annoyed I went to the DA's Office and reported that these detectives were leaning on me for money. Days passed, nothing happened. I thought that was the end of it. Then one afternoon the doorbell rang. I knew it was one of the detectives because my doorman notified me before hand that he was on the way up. He began to warn me about talking to the DA. I responded by telling him I was going back to the DA if he didn't leave. He used my bathroom, but was in there a long time, perhaps ten minutes. I imagined he was planting something. When he came out, I began to edge him to the door until he suddenly grabbed me from behind, putting his hands across my breasts. Holding me so tight, I could hardly move. All this time he was rubbing against me, toying with me, showing me who was in charge. After struggling with him a while, he finally let me loose and I virtually threw him out the door. I called the DA's office again. Just to be safe, that night a friend and I emptied everything in the bathroom to make sure I wasn't being framed.

At this point I became concerned about Clovis, because of the arrest business, the detectives and the job-hunting, I didn't have much time to spend with him. I hadn't been keeping track of him and he was growing up so fast. As a young boy he was a loner, often spending time by himself. As he grew he read a lot and listened to music. In school, he was a good student—bright, articulate, but not a class leader in a popularity sense. He was truly a beautiful child. I know all mothers say that, but in this instance it was everyone else saying it to me. He had bright blue eyes and natural straight blond hair. He could be friendly, when he wanted to be, and had a winning smile. I wanted to be sure his potential was realized, so I enrolled him in an expensive boarding school in Darien, Connecticut. That, I thought, would provide him (now twelve years old) good schooling, and also distance him from the bad elements that I seemed to currently be surrounded by.

He'd only been there a short time when my sister Terri and I went to visit. We found all the kids running around naked, clothes strewn everywhere, while the woman who owned and ran the place was off somewhere out of sight. Without a second thought we packed up Clovis and his things and took him home.

Between Clovis and my many jobs, I didn't have much of a life in the early sixties. I was dating, but only sporadically. The nightlife in New York had tapered off noticeably, in part due to the success of TV in keeping people at home. TV dinner's became the rage. Even after-hour clubs were hurting, but that's still where I was trying to make a living. I knew I couldn't hold an office job. I couldn't type or do shorthand. I couldn't go into some factory for 50 cents an hour. My new hatcheck job was now at another expensive restaurant. A lot of models hung out there, but no illegal business was transacted, so there wasn't the risk of being arrested again.

All the excitement from the arrest, job hunting, and long hours from my new job took their toll, and I was very sick for a time, and unable to work. So, I had to sell all my jewelry to pay the rent and buy food. I was trying to cope with a teenage boy who was undergoing a metamorphosis of his own. After the Darien school debacle I enrolled Clovis into St Ann's Academy, where he lived on campus. I thought this would be a good solution to keep him focused on school during the week, and then have him home for the weekends. The education he received there however certainly is not what I intended.

His best friend Peter also attended St. Ann's. Peter's mother seemed rather uninterested in where Peter was or what he was doing: I don't ever recall her visiting. He lived at the academy full time and Clovis and he spent a lot of time together. One weekend, they were in Clovis's room at my apartment when I overheard the two of them talking; my blood began to boil. "Did he touch you too," one voice asked, "Yes, he does it all the time," the other responded. I was horrified; one of the priests at the school had been sexually abusing them. No one challenged the church back then—God's wrath and all that. I immediately took Clovis out of the school and called Peter's mother, who, had no reaction.

For the next several months Peter spent the weekends at my apartment: I bought a cot for him to set up in Clovis's room because I couldn't image him there (at the school) alone. When we went to the country to spend time at a little cabin I owned. Peter would accompany us. I was never a country person. I didn't know anything about nature, but I did like the quiet getaway from time to time, with no idea that I would spend more time in the country in years to come. Upon my return to the cabin I would always find the driveway littered with garbage. "Where does this all come from?" I inquired. I was told that it must be from the "coons." The next morning at breakfast, I quickly ran towards the door when I heard the garbage trucks coming. "Where are you going Harriet," Larry asked. "To talk to the coons and straighten out this garbage problem," I insisted. "Raccoons, Harriet, I was referring to raccoons!" I felt really stupid, and never realized he was talking about animals.

You always think each problem is big, until something happens to put things in proper perspective. Clovis had already had some turbulent times in his young life, but life was about to deliver another blow. "The walls were covered in blood," he told me, tears running down his face. "The police found Peter at school, dead! They filed it as a suicide." I called Peter's mother to offer condolences, but she seemed rather unaffected. Clovis never spoke of it again.

Clovis had mentioned he'd like to study fashion design, so I enrolled him in The High School of Arts and Design, located around the corner from our apartment. It wasn't easy. Acceptance came only from recommendations, so I visited an old friend of mine working at Madison Square Garden who had some influence and Clovis was admitted. His artistic talents were very recognizable, even then. I was pleased, at first. He was doing something creative in school, and he had lots of equally creative friends. I thought maybe he would turn out to be an artist or fashion designer, working for one of those big fashion houses. I didn't realize he was destined for bigger things. He and his friends would study at the apartment, but seemingly more and more, they began fooling around. I was working late nights and began to dread coming home. Furniture got broken. I'd find liquor bottles hidden and clothes that weren't Clovis'. One morning I came home and no one was there. I became alarmed and went scouring the neighborhood, trying to remember where these other kids lived, or where they liked to hang out. I found nothing. When he finally turned up, alone, I was distraught.

Clovis was a rebellious kid, like many his age, and with me working late Clovis had the evenings to himself, and he sure *abused the privilege.* Sound familiar? Perhaps my mother was getting her wish. He answered my questions in that maddening way kids have when they don't want to tell you anything. He was at a party, he said, and forgot what time it was. After chewing him out for a few moments, I let it go. After all, he was in the position where I had placed him. If it was anyone's fault, it was mine. We had more than our share of arguments. On one occasion he shouted, "You're a terrible mother!" How was I supposed to respond to that? "You didn't come with a manual," I said, "I'm doing the best I can!" He absorbed the thought, but didn't react to it.

I had no control over him any longer, and so that's when I decided to do something very unorthodox: I let him go out on his own, at the age of 15. I found a small apartment for him in the neighborhood, close enough that I could be there quickly if he needed me, and told him he was responsible for himself. Of course, I expected he'd be back in a jiffy after a few months, willing to abide by any terms I set. It never happened. Having his own apartment just heightened his adventurous spirit. The next thing I knew he had a girlfriend living with him. Then, I found out he had a monkey—because the City Board of health was knocking on my door to tell me it had bitten everyone. I got scared over that. I had learned in Egypt that monkey bites could be fatal. Fortunately, they stepped in and took away the monkey and all the kids had to have a shot for rabies. The New York Dally News picked up on the story and Clovis found himself in the newspapers for the first time. It wouldn't be the last. He said he wanted to continue to live his own life, so I let him. We would stay in touch enough for me to help pay for his education, but he stayed mostly in his own world.

If his wild behavior wasn't enough to deal with, I also came to realize that Clovis wasn't paying the bills. Whatever money he was making from the after school jobs he had was used to buy antiques. The past due notices were piling up, so without notice, I took two of his Spanish chairs and sold them. He was dumbfounded, "I can't believe you did that," he said, "Do you know how unique those chairs were?" Actually, I didn't. Nor did I care. For most of the next year we didn't speak.

I had met Al Cardozo, a plain, quiet guy who worked as a claim adjuster for New York Life Insurance Company in New York. He grew up poor and thought poor. He was also extremely bigoted and overly religious. For example, I once told him I knew of some Maryknoll fathers who were gay. He was so enraged that he started to choke me. He was insanely jealous, very possessive, and checked up on me constantly. He also drank too much and would get nasty when drinking. I decided to stop seeing him. It was about this time that an old friend said he knew a "very nice man" he thought I would like to meet. "A really great guy," he said. He has a home in Mountain Lakes, New Jersey. I had heard this kind of thing before, of course, so I wasn't swept off my feet. What does "nice" mean, after all. I knew I could still draw men's looks when I got dolled up, so I wasn't desperate. I didn't have to be fixed up by my friends. But finally, I thought, "oh why not?" Ten days later, he called and said "You're to meet George on Saturday at 3:00 p.m. under the clock at the Biltmore." How romantic," I thought. This is where girls used to meet returning servicemen during the war, and generations of young girls met their beaus there.

So at the appointed time, on the 10th of April I was standing under the Clock, watching all the men who passed. Finally a man came up and said, "I'm George. Are you Harriet?" When I nodded, he suggested we go across the lobby to the dining room and have a sandwich. I could feel the chemistry between us right away as we looked over the menu. We both ordered ham and Swiss cheese on rye. We engaged in small talk to get through the awkwardness. When the sandwiches arrived, we both picked up a half and began to eat, only to realize the bread was stale. Neither of us said anything. We just ate them anyway.

Later in our courtship, when we were more comfortable about discussing our private thoughts, we admitted to one another that we tasted the staleness of that first sandwich we had together, but didn't want to spoil anything by commenting on it. That awkward start became a private ritual. In commemoration of our first date, on each anniversary we'd go to the Biltmore and order the same thing—ham and Swiss sandwich on stale bread. The waitress would give us one of those looks and we'd laugh.

Moments like that was a part of our relationship. We liked to tell jokes and put people on, harmlessly. We'd get in a cab and once underway, he'd say to me, "got any heroin, marijuana, or anything?" I'd say, "Not on me, it's back in the apartment." We'd get a look from the driver, then we'd laugh. We both loved to dance. We'd go to regular dances, but we'd also dance at other times: into the elevator, up the stairs, out of the apartment to the elevator. We'd play hide-and-seek on the street, with other people wondering if we were from Bellevue Hospital. Getting on the elevator, with everyone standing facing front we faced the back. We'd take long goodbyes, waving at one another when we were six feet away, and then turn around and wave from a distance until one of us was out of sight. I'm sure people thought we were really loony, but we didn't care, we were happy. I wasn't in love, but I was comfortable. My mother used to tell me that usually one person loves, and the other is loved. I preferred the latter. Year's later people on my street would stop me and tell me how much they enjoyed watching George and I carry on. He was more fun than anyone I had ever known.

Despite the slow start and stale bread we'd made an impression on one another, and George asked me to meet him the next day, for lunch at the Hotel Astor. I agreed. Before I left the apartment, I received a bouquet of beautiful silver roses. We talked a lot during that lunch and discovered our personalities were similar and compatible. We also talked about serious things—us. I told him about my previous marriage to Don and about Clovis and he told me about his 15 year old daughter Martha, who was living with his ex-wife. I noticed his jacket. "Doesn't anybody care about you?" I asked with a big smile. "Look at your coat sleeves. They're too long." No, he admitted, no one looked after him. So, after lunch I took him back to my apartment and shortened his sleeves.

When Clovis met George he liked him right away. Later, he said, "Listen, this is a real nice guy, a straight shooter. Loose all those call girls and any other seedy friends you have, and change your phone number. Play it straight with this guy, and by all means, don't go to bed with him unless he marries you!" Here I was enchanted with a new man in my life, and my seventeen-year old son was giving me dating advice. Clovis spoke with such confidence that you were compelled to listen. I had gotten out of the hatcheck business a short time before and returned to my own roots in fashion, mostly making costumes and special garments for the ex-showgirls from the Copa, Latin Quarter, and other New York clubs for reunions, charities, and other special events that required costuming. So, it wasn't difficult at this point to change my lifestyle, and I decided to follow Clovis' advise.

George's real qualities hadn't been revealed yet, at these early stages. I knew he could be fun and light-spirited. But I didn't know what else he was made of. I knew I had a pretty face and my figure was still attractive, and that's all that a lot of men looked at. Still, I sensed that George wanted to take a serious interest. And if so, I wanted to make sure he knew what kind of girl I was and what I expected of people, especially men. Before we got too serious about one another, I wanted to make some things clear. First, I asked him why we always met for lunch. Why not dinner, where we could spend a little more time together? "Are you single, George?" He explained that, "yes" he was single, but he spent weekends with his mother who was dying. She lived at his home 40 miles west of Manhattan, and each day he went home immediately after work to relieve the day nurse. She died several months later.

He also told me that he had his own advertising agency, and that among his accounts was Pan Am. He made a lot of money and he liked to spend it. (As it turned out, he especially liked to spend it on me. I liked that too.) With these preliminaries out of the way, we continued to see one another whenever we could, but always in the city. When I asked him what he wanted for his birthday, he said, "How about marrying me?" We had been going out for two months. I was surprised, but wasn't against the idea. But before committing, I had a few other things to get out in the open. Looking back, it took some nerve to say all that I did, in view of my strapped financial circumstances. But whether I was wealthy or not, I would have felt the same.

I told him I would never marry a cheap man. I'd lived alone since Murray left in 1956. I was set in my ways and I was used to certain things, including financial freedom. "I'm not going to go out and buy a fur coat, but I shouldn't have to "clear" everything first." I said that marriage should be a partnership. Everything goes into the checking account. I didn't want to have to come to him and say, "Can I have a pair of shoes?" To me, that's begging. I couldn't go that route. I'm very independent. No secrets about money. And I wanted that candor to go both ways.

Second, I said, I don't want your daughter or my son living with us if we get married. Also, people meet each other, they're crazy for one another, they're in bed and sex is everything in their lives, so they get married. A year later they are divorced because they really never got to know one another. Knowing another person takes time, and you have to give a relationship a chance. So, on vacations, we don't do things we don't like to do. You may want to go down the Klondike in a canoe; I may want to go to Vegas. But we shouldn't do them if I can't stand canoes and casinos bore you. We should learn to do together what we both like. If there's some place you want to go, and I don't, we have to compromise.

There was little need to go through all this with George. I could see he wasn't going to try to be king of the household. I knew also that beneath that easygoing attitude and friendly style there was a reassuring firmness. George was successful, bright and got along with people. His office was at East 55th Street and Madison, just down the street from me. He exercised regularly, ate sensible foods. His regular checkups showed him to be in perfect health. If this sounds cold-blooded, you have to remember that for my generation marriage was often our support and livelihood, not just a romantic gesture. I'm emotionally and intellectually self-sufficient, but I had to be sure my husband was able to support me in every sense of the word.

So we agreed to get married. On our wedding day, September 1, 1964, we had known each other for four months. George sold his house in Mountain Lakes and moved in with me. We both agreed that a Manhattan residence was the best of all possible worlds. He liked the idea that he could walk to work, and I, of course, would never give up my rent-controlled apartment. But there was an ugly preamble. Al was not going to give up, when he heard I was seeing George, he stalked me, called in the middle of the night but wouldn't say anything; he just sat on the phone breathing heavily. I'd come home and he'd be hiding in the phone booth on the corner, or sitting on the steps across from my apartment. He threatened to throw acid in my face, saying that no one would want me after that. Finally, I was so afraid of him that I told George, and he went to the precinct in our neighborhood and filed a report, and that seemed to be the end of it.

CHAPTER 18

A Rising Son, a Coty and Cloudy Skies

The boy became a man right before my eyes. Did your parents ever mention that you should cherish every moment of your life because time flies? Well, they were right, it does. But of course most of us say, "yeah, yeah," and roll our eyes. We seem to only learn from our own experiences, not those who came before us. Think of how wise we'd all be if we had listened to our elders. My son was no different and he had more than his share of experiences to learn from. After the death of his father he and I returned to New York City and had survived some extreme ups and downs. He was just a toddler back then, but even so, I'm sure that he retained some awareness of what was occurring— even if only by osmosis.

Clovis had ideas for fashion early on though I never tuned into it being anything more than a temporary diversion. Even as far back as the military academy, I can now recall finding him off on his own, under a tree, arranging the leaves in patterns on the ground. Years later I would arrive home from work to see brown paper bags designed with drawings, and later, his clothes decorated with accessories from my sewing room.

By the age of 18 he was drawn for a time to the visual arts, and worked with fashion photographer Ruspolli Rodigues. He even contributed to the famous "Hair" poster, one of the more memorable graphics of that era. But, even at that undecided point in his life, Clovis' realized ambitions were elsewhere— with his first love, fashion. He'd borrow expensive women's clothes from Bill Blass and Oscar de la Renta to use in his photography, and then, realized that photography bored him. It was the styling he enjoyed. Clovis was just a kid with a sense of fashion, a dream, and virtually no money. But, he had determination and that other essential element: talent.

While attending Columbia University he took an apartment on Bank Street, and then later moved to the top floor of a townhouse on 58th Street, both the courtesy of a very conservative southern gentleman named Mr. Leroy Love. I only found out about Leroy shortly before whatever was between them, dissolved. It was on the top floor of that townhouse that Clovis began his business. He bought a few sewing machines and began making garments. But Clovis was young, still in his late teens. I wanted to know who this Leroy Love was, and why he was buying expensive gifts for my son. I grabbed Clovis and we waited at the Townhouse for Leroy. By the look in Clovis's eye I knew that the man approaching must be him. "What are you going to say to him," Clovis asked. "Whatever I decide to," I said. I must say that Leroy was indeed a gentleman, and very easy to like. Clovis was already planning to move out of the Townhouse and take a loft on 19th Street by that time, so I didn't press. It would be several years later before I would see Leroy again, and he invited me for dinner on a few occasions. It was enjoyable, but I never did find out whether the connection between he and Clovis was romantic, or paternal in nature.

The loft on 19th street was like a hippie, fashion commune. "We were children of the sixties," a friend said when describing the scene there. "On any given day you could walk in and see a designer cutting patterns in one corner—whether it was clothing, belts, hats, or handbags—couples having sex, and people getting high—all side by side in the open loft." All the designers were broke and Clovis's loft was where they would congregate, sometimes staying for days or weeks at a time. Again, I found myself footing the rent, and one day just walked in and snapped. "Everybody, if you're not paying rent, get out!" Of course they just looked at me as if I was speaking a foreign language. Clovis pulled me aside and was aghast that I could do such a thing. I told him that if he didn't want to collect rent from them, then perhaps he should pay the bills himself. Nothing came of it. Within days the activity in the loft was right back to the usual scene.

While Clovis was living in his commune styled loft George bought a three-acre piece of property at Lake Mohawk in Sparta, a lovely wooded area in Northwest, New Jersey, near the Pennsylvania Border and the Delaware water gap. Our plan was to pull down the existing old house there, and build a country home that would be our escape on weekends all year round; a place to entertain in grand fashion. There was a big, beautiful tree in the center of the property, where we wanted the house to be. So, we built the house around it, and let the tree become the centerpiece of conversation. When the house was finished, it went up through a skylight. We added an Olympic size pool, a cabana house and a huge patio off the kitchen. We named the house

Wrightopia and planned special parties with special menus we created from things we learned in our cooking classes back in Manhattan. The Kitchen was 20x20 and had a fireplace, a place our guests would always congregate. We'd stop at the bakery on 9th Avenue in New York City and get all the cakes and breads for the weekend, and all our country friends would anxiously be waiting our arrival on Friday night.

On Saturday, the group would come over at noon, sit around the pool, have lunch and drinks on the patio and swim. At the end of the day, they'd go home to dress and come back for dinner and a fun evening. We inherited an old pump organ that everyone stood around while they sang and George played. On Sunday morning, everyone came back for a huge breakfast that George would cook, and then later in the day we would head back to New York. George had two brothers, Sterling, a retired lieutenant general in the Army lived in Virginia, and Richard was head of the airport facilities for American Airlines in Louisville, Kentucky. We visited back and forth constantly.

During the week, we went to school together. Our entire week was filled with self-education: Monday was tap dancing, Tuesday was art, Wednesday was cooking school, and Thursday was woodworking. Friday evenings we'd be off to Lake Mohawk, to return Sunday evening. We followed this routine for years, and never found it boring. The classes changed but never our interest in trying new things together. George also liked to surprise me by leaving little love notes everywhere. I'd find one in the coffee can in the morning, or under the coffee cup, or in the medicine chest. Any place he knew I would look was a likely place for a note:

- *"Darlingist, you are the only person that I have ever loved. You are the personification of all the attributes that I want. With you I am the happiest guy in the world—without you, the most miserable,*

Or this one,

- *"My darling Sweetheart Precious Adorable, I am the luckiest guy in the world to be married to you. Together we can do anything. I worship you. Geo."*

If my husband was intelligent and kind, I would have to say that my son was brilliant and complex. I imagine he developed his social skills at an early age, doing the nightclub circuit with Murray. He was around wealthy people and saw how they dressed. He learned how to greet people, and how to rebuff them. Close friends would later say, "There's a driving force behind Clovis. He gives out a tremendous amount of energy and has definite likes and dislikes. He is refreshingly honest, witty, and bitchy—sometimes at the same time. He makes you his confidante after he insults you." He became a student of human behavior, and began to learn how to zone in on what made a person tick. He would digest a book of psychology—and then put it to practical use. Later, it was common to see him reading two books at the same time, one in each hand. "He understood people. And combined with his boyish charm and fun loving nature, people were putty in his hands," Rosie said. She was the only person to ever live with Clovis in his adult years (on and off for a total of six years).

She said of Clovis that he was the real Holly Golightly. He exuded charm, grace and style, with an eclectic off beat way about him. He did what he liked, wore what he liked, and was as he chose to be—without concern about what people would think. He'd wear the most unconventional things, and rather than question him, people would emulate him. He could go weeks, or months, wearing nothing but black, then switch—without warning or explanation—to Chinese, or purple or pink. He was greatly influenced by the colors and styles of Harlem in those early days. Later, on a trip to China, he returned with black silk jackets for everyone. To this day photographer Roxanne Lowit still wears Chinese jackets as her "fashion-less" as a "fashion statement" signature style; a testament to the Clovis influence. This was just one of those quirky little things that made Clovis unique. He was one of—if not the first—man to carry a handbag, and made turquoise jewelry for men popular. His lifestyle was on the go around the clock, because he loved life, and people—well, some people.

Clovis knew what he wanted in those early days and he began getting his own basic training, you might say, looking for ways to express his creative urges. The first design he brought to the public was a great success: designer T—shirts—do you remember that? At that time, if you mentioned T-shirts, people would think of undershirts, not outerwear. Working in a friend's summer cottage on Fire Island, the trendy place to be back then, Clovis took the T-idea and brought it to new levels. He designed baby T-shirts first, with block lettering that said things like, "I Love You," "I'm a Boy," or "I'm a Girl" woven into the fabrics. These were the first products that would prove to be profitable for Clovis during the next few years.

After he had made a bunch of T-shirts, cutting and sewing them himself, he put them in a shopping bag and took them around to the department stores: Bloomingdale's, Macy's, Lord & Taylor, Saks, plus the smart boutiques. Bendel's, the chic store on Manhattan's 57th Street told him that "Spanish clothes were in, not your clothes," he later recalled. He didn't listen. He believed he had a winner. Finally Bloomingdale's agreed to display his shirts and proved him right. His first order was $4500, and they sold as fast as he could deliver them. Lord & Taylor and Capezio soon followed, and the rest, as they say, is history.

Things were quickly picking up speed and Clovis was actually generating money from his designs. From that point on, he couldn't make his garments fast enough. Friends helped by making sales calls, taking orders and delivering merchandise. But, this was fast evolving from a start up boutique enterprise to a full-blown business. He hired people to sew and moved his operation into a loft at 333 Park Ave south, even though cash flow was still tight. The new loft had 25' ceilings, and would serve as living quarters, party commune, and business center. The neighborhood was downtrodden; with hookers walking the street at night, who for $10 would provide a little roadside service on their knees to anyone in a passing car that chose to stop. Clovis was fascinated with them. He had the ability to look past the obvious, and could see in them a boldness, a sense of style all their own. He would invite them to the loft regularly. Not for sex, but just to get to know them, and understand them. Sometimes they would partake in his late night impromptu fashion shows.

Meanwhile, he was sure that he could do a booming business if he could mass-produce his clothes. He needed money, but he didn't want charity. He wanted what any other young businessman sought: working capital. Clovis approached George for loans on two separate occasions. He then bought his fabrics, turned out his goods, profited, repaid George and was on his way to the next level. But he was overwhelmed with all the facets of the business, and wanted to keep his focus on the designing and promoting. A friend, furniture designer Angelo Donghia, suggested that he become Clovis's manager. Being friends, and lovers, Clovis trusted him completely. He was heart-broken to eventually learn that Angelo was running his own business, using Clovis's money. Not that Angelo needed it; he was very successful in his own right. But some people just can't help taking what appears to be available for the taking.

Clovis was focused on bigger things. He organized his first fashion show in 1972, and broke all the rules. He opted for rock music, and in the words of Stuart Kreisler (a Brooklyn born, Seventh Avenue wizard, who found his niche by handling the manufacture and distribution of products by various designers) "Clovis' was the first fashion show I had ever seen that was literally choreographed—it was an event". He would later tell journalists, "Clovis was contemporary fashion, and the term 'contemporary' came from him. We cut our deal on a proposition I made during that first show, which was written on a pack of matches. In six months, Clovis was not "in" fashion, he had "become" a fashion" he said. Stuart, who already had several successful designers and would add Ralph Lauren to his stable, would provide Clovis the stability and infrastructure he needed to grow his business, rapidly.

Original and unique in everything he did, Clovis opted to use mostly black models in that first show. No other designer had ever used black models before, and especially in such a dominating way. Now it's common practice. But Clovis was like that, he did whatever his instincts told him to do, regardless of what others said or thought. He had vision and knew what he wanted. He had no time or patience for those that didn't get it. The journalist Eugenia Shepard wrote that Clovis," made history in his first collection."

Indeed, his face became a familiar fixture on the fashion pages of newspapers and magazines nationwide. Syndicated columns brought his style and his fashion views to an ever-widening audience of young workingwomen. Soon, he would also be designing clothes for celebrities like Diana Ross, Rona Barrett, Kay Ballard, the Alvin Alley dancers, Gladys Knight, and others. The Broadway producer/writer Jerry Herman (known for Hello Dolly, Mame, La Cage aux Follies, and others) contracted Clovis on several occasions to design costumes for various stage characters in his plays. I personally liked Jerry very much.

Clovis only had two committed relationships, and with both, he always maintained a separate apartment: he didn't co-habitat with anyone. Except for Rosie. But they were never romantically involved; they were friends, and total opposites. She liked fashion, but wasn't in fashion. She laughs and says she was, "his small non interested muse." They had a great time together on 19th street, and after she went traveling and dropped out of sight for two years, Clovis tracked her down at her parent's house in Washington Heights. "What are you doing at

Kay Ballard & Clovis

your parents house? You just traveled the world. While you've been gone lot's has happened. I won the designers Coty Critics Award and I'm making lots of money. Pack your bags and get down here right away!" He gave her the address and hung up.

When she arrived they picked up where they left off. The new loft was larger, and the parties more extravagant but nothing else had changed. They would frequent Max's Kansas City, a club made famous by the Andy Warhol crowd during the 1970s, and sleep on an average of three hours a night. Clovis worked as hard as he played. Details bored him, but he would stay up late at night working on designs while he watched old movies. Clovis and Rosie had little in common other than those old movies, having fun, and being naked. Both were comfortable lounging around the apartment, or sitting in the hot tub: nude. If someone happened to stop by—or even if it was a guest he invited

Clovis Ruffin 1970s

over—Clovis might climb out of the hot tub and answer the door naked if the mood struck him to do so. Sometimes it was just to shock people, to see how they'd react to the totally unexpected. After a few conversations at Studio 54, Clovis struck up a friendship with Nikki Haskell and invited her to his apartment. When she arrived he answered the door totally naked. She didn't say anything about that. They sat on the couch and talked for a while. Then she got up and left. "He never mentioned it again, and neither did I," she said.

Clovis's career had taken off like a rocket and it showed no signs of slowing down. My own connections with "show business" had faded years earlier, but since signing with Stuart Chrysler, Clovis now needed to produce a fashion show to introduce a new line every year. So, I was hired as an assistant for the shows, which became almost a full time job. When one show ended, we started preparing for next year. Clovis gave me a new life, and I made the most of it. My job was to shop for accessories, such as ribbons, hats, flowers, bows, seamed stockings, fans, and shoes (usually 10 pairs at a time) for the models on the runway. I made sure that their makeup was flawless and that all the color coordinated items were in place, as well as confirm that the program information matched the schedule of what would be shown. The lighting program had to be checked, because each garment had its own, designed to show off that item's features to best advantage. Some shows had as many as 1,000 people in the audience, not all of them buyers. These shows attracted fashion writers, editors, celebrities known for their fashion tastes, newspaper and magazine columnists who knew that gossip was an integral by-product of the fashion industry.

Clovis and I developed a weekly ritual. Most every Saturday, we'd board a bus to East 86th Street and Madison, get off, and work our way back to 59th Street to see what the fashion shops were featuring. He'd hold up a dress and say, "What'd you think?" or "How's this look?" He'd peruse a rack of dresses and say, "Hmm…I wonder what Harriet would wear?" If you didn't recognize Clovis, or realize that he was some kind of designer, and you saw us doing this you'd wonder what our game was—a young, blond hunk and a five-foot, no longer 21 year old lady, holding up dresses for one another. I'm sure we amused many. We had a great time. We'd pick out and laugh at or admire the same things. We really enjoyed each other's company and had become friends, and were also developing the fun of being mother and son that eluded us earlier in life.

As his assistant, I maintained regular hours, but as his mother I was on call 24x7. Late one night the phone rang and I answered it, still sleepy. "You have to come down here right away," he said. I looked at the clock and it was 1:00 AM. Outside the window I could see that it was still snowing. He didn't live around the corner any longer, and the ride to his penthouse at Abington Square in the Village was a long one. Of course the freezing cold made it seem even longer. "Come down quickly and bring your sewing machine...hurry!" he insisted—then he hung up. I got dressed, grabbed my sewing machine and went out into the cold to get a cab. When I arrived at his apartment, Clovis was in the middle of the room. He had pulled down all the curtains on his huge windows, laid them out on the floor, and was cutting them according to some pattern he had devised in his head. He was kind of frenzied in that way that creative people can get, and needed me to sew the pieces together. At 5 a.m. I left, having assembled everything. I didn't think any more of it—he said he wanted some things to show somebody immediately, etc.

Weeks later, I was sitting front row at a show, and I see Clovis' curtains strutting the runway. They looked terrific! From behind the curtain I could see a pair of eyes peeking out at me from the stage. It was Clovis, of course, waiting to see the surprise on my face when I saw the garments make their appearance. When I saw him, he raised two fingers in a V sign and winked at me. Our time together wasn't all work. Clovis and I had dinner together often, with me sometimes as a third party; if Clovis had a date I'd go home after dinner, and Clovis and his date—who often was a public person in those 1970's soirees—would go dancing or to a show. Sometimes he would include me at parties, nightclubs and events, and it reminded me of the old days when I ran with the nightclub circuit crowd.

Though we saw a lot of each other we weren't inseparable. We each had our own lives. By the mid 1970s I co-founded the World Famous Copacabana Girls Inc., a non-profit organization that consisted of one hundred and fifty Copa girls representing all the different decades. Some years earlier a young club owner bought the rights to the Copacabana name and reopened the club in it's original location. Shortly after, with the supper club crowd long gone, it was converted into a disco bar, with a mirrored ball on the ceiling. I thought it was tacky. But, after it closed, the club was moved—in yet another attempt to revive the Copa name—to West 57th Street and 10th Ave. On behalf of *The World Famous*

Otto & Harriet

Copacabana Girls Inc., I organized many benefits there for aids and other charitable events that attracted such dignitaries as Mayor Beame, Henny Youngman, Michael Todd, Liz Taylor, Robert Mitchum, Joan Crawford and the then famous film director Otto Preminger, to name a few. To say the owner of the Copa, John Juliano, was accommodating would be a drastic understatement. He always went out of his way to help me, and supported my efforts and

Copa Girls Revival

our organizations objects whenever it was requested. John is one of those rare people that you feel fortunate to meet, and we became good friends.

Clovis and his friends would often attend some of these functions as well, and on one occasion he picked up the phone in our hour of need and in just 4 hours sold 175 tickets that we were unable to. They say you can't go home again, but suddenly I found myself surrounded by memories of days passed: the Copa, famous people, and lots of glitz and glamour. But, I didn't just get to remember it; I got to relive it. Peter Allen did a special performance of his hit song, "I Go To Rio" at the Waldorf Astoria Hotel. Together with Paula Lemont (a Copa girl from 1969) and three other Copa girls dressed in our famous Copa costumes, we got to be in the chorus line one more time.

From the hallway one morning George asked me where I wanted to eat that night, and then tapped danced into the elevator and threw me a kiss saying, "Love you." He walked a few blocks to his office and collapsed of a massive heart attack. After 45 minutes he couldn't be revived. I was devastated. Clovis took care of everything. So, once again, the bottom fell out, and I was facing yet another beginning. This time however, I had Clovis to help me through, and for the first time wasn't starting from the bottom. I kept those little spontaneous notes George wrote me, and when I read them it always brings a smile to my face. It reminds me time after time how wonderful it was to have a man who loved me. We were about as happy a couple as you could imagine. I may not have had the same passion for George that I did for Don, but I loved being with, and being loved by him.

By the late 1970s there was no club, anywhere, as famous as Studio 54 in New York City. It was a phenomenon, the "in" place to be. And, I was there to see it first hand, the benefit of a son with a fast rising star. Even though it wasn't my cup of tea, it was exciting, eventful and always energetic. It was like a ride at

Disney land, only with sex and drugs. The music was loud and pounding, not at all like the softer music of the 40s and 50s that I liked. To me this new music was just noise. But the crowds sure loved it. People waited on lines for hours with the hope of getting into Studio 54. And if you weren't well known or a celebrity, you had better be dressed in some fabulous outfit to convince the doorman that you were worthy of entrance, or you would be bluntly turned away. Celebrities were everywhere; on the dance floor and in the VIP balcony, engaging in sex and drugs—lot's of drugs. I would see Halston there with young men, almost incoherent. He wasn't the only one; there were other celebrities doing drugs, and/or having sex: straight, gay, and everything in between. It was a time of excess.

Nikki Haskel was the host of a Manhattan cable show, on location inside Studio 54 (which reminded me of the days when Barry Gray hosted his radio show from within the Copacabana, 35+ years earlier). She and Clovis had chemistry almost immediately. You could see it, feel it, just by being near them—and boy, could they dance. When Clovis and Nikki took the floor they were like a force that compelled people to stop what they were doing and watch. I really believe Nikki loved Clovis and would have married him had he asked. He had once confided in me that he was strongly consider-ing doing just that. He had thoughts of con-verting one of his lofts into a home for them, but then abruptly, for whatever reason,

Nikki & Clovis

changed his mind. I never heard any more about it but I think he just wasn't the marrying type, and wanted to stay single. To this day she refers to me as her mother-in-law, and I love her as if I was. She went on to build a very successful business and was listed as US Magazines "It Girl" of 2002. She is a self-made woman, and I have nothing but love and respect for her. She attended my most recent birthday in 2005, and as a surprise picked up the tab for me and the other fourteen guests. "I have it and I love you, why shouldn't I pay for it." She said. I thought that was wonderful.

Success changed Clovis's lifestyle, but it didn't change him. An interview in 1978 said: "In 1973, he was the youngest designer ever to win the prestigious Coty award, which you could compare to an Oscar—for his concept of "fash-ion at a price." Today at age 30, he is recognized as one of the country's most important young designers of dresses, knits, handbags, travel cases, and loungewear. Tall, slender, agile and dashingly handsome, Clovis Ruffin seems to be singularly unaffected by the pressures of his job, as we sit talking in his large 7th Avenue headquarters. In spite of his rapid rise in the world of fashion, Clovis has lost none of his boyish playfulness or sense of humor."

When asked about fashion, he tends to be highly opinionated. "American designers are more limited than European designers in what they can get away with," he once told a reporter. "The Europeans are allowed to do anything. They show day-glo underwear with see-through raincoats, feather hats, snakes. But they also take much more pride in their craftsmanship. Here, in America, they don't care. Manufacturers just want to make a lot of money and then get out of the business. If they could make money by processing Q-tips they would. In Europe, they want to pass the business on to their sons. In America, everybody wants to be someone else!" But on other subjects, such as food, he is likely to laugh his way through an answer that is pure entertainment. "I hate to cook. I'd rather not eat than cook. You don't meet anybody in the kitchen. I decided years ago that I was never going to cook again. I emptied my kitchen cupboards; I put all my winter clothes in there. My oven is full of T-shirts and bathing suits. I'm the only person in New York who never complains about not having any closet space." That's vintage Clovis the reporter noted.

To those he liked, he was generous. I've always hated a cheap person. If I can't do something first class, such as take a vacation or buy a new outfit—I don't want to do it. He was the same way; I guess the apple didn't fall far from the tree. He was a great dresser himself and preferred Armani. Nikki would often have him on her show, as a model (and co-commentator). "He had a natural ability for commentary and interviewing," she remembers. He wanted those around him to look their best too. So he would splurge on friends and family, and would think nothing of buying me a $4500 Fabrice dress, or jewelry and fur coats. Of course, that never stopped the designer Halston from taking cheap shots at me. He lived in the Penthouse in my building, where Elsa Peretti (a famous jewelry designer for Tiffany and others) lives now. One day I ran into him in the hallway. He looked me up and down, and said, "Why don't you get Clovis to dress you." Weeks later, he was present at a cocktail party I attended, and he saw me across the room. I was wearing a beautiful satin brocade suit, which I could tell he was impressed with. "Is that a Clovis suit?" he asked. Just to put him on I said, "No, I bought it at the Salvation Army for $3.95, do you like it?" He turned and walked away in a huff, obviously annoyed. I didn't care, because on a personal level I never liked him anyway. He was a very pretentious, conceited, and nasty man.

Life was great! My son was famous, successful and happy, what else could a mother hope for? A by-product of his fame kept me active in clubs and parties, and gave me the opportunity to stay active in the world of fashion, what more could I ask for? You would think that with the life I had led so far, I could meet any challenge head on, right? Wrong! Nothing in my life could have prepared me for what was to come next. Clovis called and sounded tentative, "meet me for lunch, I have something to tell you."

He spent the summers in the Hamptons, where he was a popular guest at the summerhouse of his friend Egon Von Furstenberg. It was during the previous summer that he contracted Lyme disease there, and I was worried that the condition had worsened. I met him at the restaurant, and he was unusually somber. He looked at me from across the table and said, "I have aids." I felt as though I had just been stabbed in the heart. The pain was sharp and swift. I couldn't speak. I didn't say anything, I just cried. How do you ever prepare for such a thing? I could only wonder why? Hadn't life dealt me enough blows? He said he wanted to come live with me. So we put his furniture, and some of mine in storage, and converted my living room to a private room for him. Virtually no one knew about his illness—don't forget, in those days the general public knew very little about AIDS, and even the victims themselves were ignorant. Everyone believed he was fighting the Lyme disease, which was quite debilitating in it's own right.

For the first year, we got through somewhat easily. He was noticeably thin, but continued to stay active, seeing friends and going out. Although he was in no condition to deal with his fashion design business, he could do certain kinds of work at home. Stuart Kreisler—who I have a special place in my heart for—remained a true friend to Clovis. He'd call or stop in to see how he was doing quite often, and continued to find Clovis different jobs—a notable job being the design of a house interior on Long Island. Clovis also designed the den and bathroom for Sammy Davis Jr. and Altovise. Friends would say Clovis deconstructed fashion. He broke it down, and created something new. He could be in a room not more than five minutes, and before you knew it he was moving furniture. They often said he was a closeted interior designer at heart. He also found work as a fashion consultant, which kept him creatively active, and I would see him many nights sitting up in bed sketching.

By the second year, he was noticeably weaker. For a time he worked as much as he could, and his close friends came to visit. I would arrange for a beautician to come in and do his hair and keep him well groomed. But as the months passed, he became more and more feeble, eventually unable to speak or walk. He spent his waking hours in a wheelchair, and shortly after I had to feed and diaper him. The boy that became a man before my eyes was now wasting away before them. He didn't want anyone to see him any longer, and I didn't talk to anyone about Clovis. If pushed, I would say something about the Lyme disease. AIDS was still a mystery, and people were uncomfortable discussing it. He would soon be cut off from everyone except me. For the rest of the year, I never left the house. If he needed anything I was there to get it, or I would have it sent up.

We talked a lot in those two years, and I cared for him emotionally in ways I didn't, or couldn't, when he was a boy. I never considered that Clovis might have preferred to struggle with me in New York City, rather than live in high style overseas. I guess my thoughts were always practical: what's best, what's doable, what's not. Kids however, only remember that you didn't want them around. I never did like kids, but I always thought I was doing what was in his best interest, though, who knows, maybe I was doing what was in mine. He would tease me, privately and publicly, that I was the "worst" mother. But by that time he said it in a way that I, and everyone else, knew he loved me regardless of any motherly shortcomings. I guess it was his way of letting me know that he didn't agree with every decision I made. At a time like this you reflect on missed opportunities.

The one thing I believe I did very well as a mother was allow my son to be whom he choose to be. At an early age—probably when Clovis was four or five—I recognized that he had, what I perceived to be, homosexual tendencies, which is difficult for any mother to face. You have ideas who your children will grow up to be. But, they have an identity all there own, even at an early age, and a parent can either embrace or suffocate it. The urge to work in fashion must have been somewhat clandestine for Clovis when he was young; he didn't talk about it, and outside the apartment he didn't express his fashion interests. "When you're growing up you don't tell people you're thinking clothes and fashion," he told a journalist.

Looking back I imagine that he was worried about being labeled: kids can be cruel, and a boy in the '60s playing with fashion would have been a red flag for cruel kids. I chose to embrace and love him for who ever he wanted to be, rather than try to mold him into who I thought he should be. I sat him down when he was about seven years old, and said, "Whatever life you choose is yours to live. I made my choices in life, and I will support yours—whatever they may be." There was a silent moment of clarity; we understood each other. It was never mentioned again. I can only hope that my ability to love him unconditionally made up for whatever other shortcomings I may have had.

Finally, when I had to call an ambulance and have him taken to Cabrini Hospital, he couldn't even keep his eyes open; he weighed 90 pounds. I kept a vigil at the hospital, talking to him, squeezing his hand, and praying that he knew I was beside him till the end. Four days later, on April 7, 1992, he died. I lost my son, and my best friend. He was 46 years old and taken from me too soon. No parent should have to bury his or her child. I've sat at my dinning room table on many occasions and replayed his life through my mind, consumed with emotion. Life can be so unfair.

Note: The Fashion Institute of Technology located in New York City now houses Clovis' personal papers and design files.

CHAPTER 19

I Don't Picnic

I heard the words, "It's time Mrs. Wright," which snapped me out of my daydream. Stuart Kreisler took my hand as we entered the chapel where 350 people had gathered to pay their final respects to Clovis: it seemed as though all of 7th Ave. took an unofficial holiday to be there. As I entered I heard a gasp from the crowd when they saw me. The chapel was full, and people were spilling out into the street. It was a beautiful service, though I can't recall all of the details. I do remember that I didn't want the service to be somber and sad. Clovis wouldn't have wanted that. People recounted stories and memories; like the time Clovis and a friend were stranded at a biker bar when their car broke down. The playoffs of one sport or another was on television and Clovis whispered, "Do you think we could ask them to put on the Golden Girls?" Other friends got up to speak, entertain, and give tribute: it was a celebration of his life. Another said, "I'm sure Clovis is looking down on us right now and smiling. Of course he's also critiquing everyone—she looks fabulous, he looks smart, oh honey loose some weight." I could almost hear him saying, "isn't that attractive," an inside joke we had, and it made me smile. Stuart gave a reception at the Mark Hotel uptown afterwards. It was very elegant.

You can rationalize that life goes on, but sometimes your heart and soul doesn't want to listen. I was numb and still in disbelief. I needed a diversion. I began to design hats again, something I hadn't done since the days sitting in my mother's kitchen. I've probably made more than fifty in the past 10 years. You rarely see me these days without wearing one of them: the color Pink and hats have become my fashion statement. My other diversion was traveling. I never really knew if I was running towards something, or moving away from painful memories of loss, but I kept moving nonetheless. Traveling was not new to me. I had previously been to Paris many times, Athens, Germany, Sweden, Norway, and on a trip with Roz, toured Japan, Hong Kong, Singapore,

Bali and many of the other South Pacific Islands, not to mention the Caribbean with Jose Ferrer. Looking back it seems like such a blur sometimes. But there were many places I adored, and adventures that developed—some good, some not.

I returned to Paris several times because I had good memories there, and loved the food, the nightlife, and even the architecture—something that didn't usually capture my attention. And with all the hoopla, I never had a problem with the Parisians. It has been said that they don't like American tourists, and if you don't speak the language they like you even less. But, I never found that to be true. I could always find someone who spoke English—which was good, because it's the only language I speak—except for three words I learned from Don in Norwegian: I love you.

Language barriers never stopped me from communicating. People would often say they don't speak English, but they always seemed to know what I meant when I keep right on talking to them. Despite the fact that I have been to Buenos Aires, Argentina eighteen times (I go every year on my birthday), I still don't speak a word of Spanish. My first trip there was with my friend Larry—the one who educated me about the "coons." We traveled as couriers, carrying diplomatic pouches, in exchange for free airline tickets. We did this twice. Then, on a third excursion, we rented an apartment for a week, but never stayed there. There were no sheets on the beds, or any amenities. That's like being at home, not on vacation. So after the first night we checked into the Alvear Palace Hotel, the Argentine equivalent to New York City's Plaza Hotel. It was New Year's Eve, so we decided to splurge. Everything was magnificent; it was as though we entered the land of lords and ladies and we partied till dawn.

We didn't want to go back to the apartment, but couldn't afford to stay at the Alvear Palace. We crossed the street and went to smaller hotel called the Ulysses Hotel only to discover that it too was expensive. I met the manager, a Hollywood handsome man named Carlos. He was very sweet and we hit it off right away. Through his extremely broken English, he told me to meet him after work and he would show me a very nice hotel in the area that was much less expensive. When I tell friends that this is how we met they shutter, "How did you know he wasn't trying to set you up, to rob you?" I tell them, "I just knew." Carlos took me to the Apart Recoleta, and I've been staying there—in the same room—every year since. I've developed a close friendship with Carlos and his circle of friends: Ricardo, Miguel, Eve, Adela, Charley, Norma, Sandra and most recently Isaac. They are a wonderful group of people who I love like family. Each year they never fail to host a birthday party for me. These days Buenos Aires is my favorite city, especially since Paris seems to have lost the nightlife that I loved so much. And though it is still a stunning city visually, with a Brasserie on every corner, for me, it has lost it's magic.

I still like France, and travel to Nice occasionally. I went there with Helen in 2002 and we toured the French Riviera, also known as Cote d'Azur, or blue coast, which includes; Cannes, Nice, Antibes, Monaco and St. Tropez. Everything in Nice is within walking distance. There's a pedestrian mall for shopping and great dining—my two favorite things. We stayed right by the water at the Beau Rivage, and ate lunch everyday in the outdoor restaurant overlooking the Mediterranean. When we reached St. Tropez, I spotted Ivana Trump's yacht, and went to see if she was onboard. I explained to the deck mate who I was, and within minutes she came ashore. She was delightful, and we spoke for a while.

When Ivana was organizing the grand opening for one of Donald's new hotels in Atlantic City, Nikki (Haskell) had suggested to her to have Clovis organize a fashion show for the event. He did, and that's how they first met. I also met Donald during a party celebration for his football team, the New Jersey Generals, which was in the now defunct USA Football League. Clovis had designed the cheerleader outfits and called me one night and said, "get dressed and get over to Trump Tower, there's a party and you'll love it. Go to the side door." I did, and when I knocked, Donald opened the door. I explained who I was and he was so sweet and attentive to me. "What kind of coat is that, I've never seen it before," he asked. "Monkey fur," I said. He then escorted me to a table, and personally brought me a glass of wine. We sat and talked for a while and he couldn't have been nicer.

As we were leaving Ivana's yacht, she suggested that Helen and I go to Ez, in the mountains above Nice. To any lover's reading this book, Ez is the most romantic place I've ever seen. Venice is another romantic city that I enjoyed very much. And, everyone should see Rome, if only once, which was enough for me. Amongst my travels I even ended up in Mexico, via McAllen Texas: not one of my better experiences.

I had met a handsome fellow who was a member of my travel club. He invited me to come to Texas; I thought, why not? He met me at the airport and we proceeded to the hotel; I got checked in, and he had my bags brought to the room. But, when the bellhop arrived, he had more bags than I brought. I politely protested to my host, saying, "This is not part of our arrangement." He didn't want to hear it, and proceeded to unpack. From one of his bags he was taking out food; fruit, cereal and such. "What's that?" I asked. "Breakfast," he said candidly. "I looked at him, now getting annoyed, and told him, "I don't picnic!" But he shot back, "then you don't eat." What seemed like such a nice man months earlier now seemed to be a real life buckaroo? I calmed down and went to the hotel restaurant to have dinner and contemplate my next move—alone.

Luckily, the room was large, and there were two beds. But I still sat up most of the night, fully clothed. I had that eerie, something-is-not-right feeling, but I couldn't do anything about it until the morning. By the time he awoke, I had already been to the front desk to inquire about getting a flight back to New York that day. No luck, as it turns out, the airline didn't have a flight out until Monday. Two more nights: I couldn't bare the thought of it.

As he was getting dressed he seemed a bit more normal in the daylight. Perhaps I over reacted. He said we got off to a bad start, and suggested a day trip to Mexico, just south of McAllen. I agreed. The town was nice; I liked it. There were lots of crafts and Mexican knick-knack's to look at, and I love to shop. On the way back to McAllen he handed me an apple. "What's this," I asked, and he replied, 'Lunch." Back to groceries, I thought. At the hotel I ate alone again in the restaurant that night. I waited anxiously for the morning, and at the crack of dawn I went to the airport, requesting a flight to get home. I was told the same thing that the hotel told me; the next plane was Monday. I pleaded with them, "please, get me on another airline." I explained my circumstances, and they did in fact find another airline. Back in the hotel room, with my bags now packed and ready to go, I decided to take a bath and freshen up rather than sit and watch the clock. I locked the door and slid into the tub for a hot soak.

Refreshed and relaxed, I had just gotten out of the tub and dressed when I heard a knock on the door. I opened it and there was my host, naked, holding his penis. With an eerie grin on his face, he said, "How would you like a piece of this?" I was horrified! I called him a degenerate and said he was lucky I didn't have him arrested. Lucky for him, I said, I was leaving for the airport because I had a flight out that day. I went for the phone to call a cab and he apologized and insisted that he would drive me. I agreed. Once in the car I had a pang of fear, but when I saw the airport getting larger through the car window I was truly relieved. He popped the trunk and I prepared to get out. Just then he quickly locked the doors saying, "You can't go yet," and got out of the car to close the trunk.

Panic came over me again and my mind began to race. I quickly grabbed my lipstick and wrote HELP on the windows. After quite a fuss that began to draw some attention, he opened the door and let me out. I hurried to the gate area to wait for my flight with him tagging along, insisting that it was all a misunderstanding. "Let's go back to the hotel," he said and grabbed me by the arm. "If you do not let go of me right now I'll scream," I told him. Five seconds later that's just what I did and employees from the airline rushed over and he quickly released me. I was so distraught that the airline allowed me to board the plane right then, before the actual boarding process began. Inside the plane, the stewardess told me later that he told her, "Watch over Harriet for me." I still get chills just thinking about the incident.

He reminded of Al, that half a psychopath that stalked me when I was dating George. A year or so after George died my friend Mary Ellen and I had just finished dinner and stopped at a little bar to have a nightcap. Lo and behold, I came face to face with Al: he was the bartender. At first I didn't recognize him. He had lost his looks and had a protruding stomach. "You don't remember me do you?" he asked. "It's me, Al. I've spent the last 16 years planning on how to murder you." It was a terrorizing feeling when I realized who he was. He went on to say that he had tapes he saved all these years of us in bed together from a tape recorder that was hidden under the bed. I had ruined his life, he said, and he was going to ruin mine. People use the word psychopath rather loosely, but this man was indeed a psychopath. I left the bar knowing that given the chance, he would harm me. A short time later I was relieved to learn that he shot himself; he was dying of cirrhosis of the liver.

But, I had good times too. After George had died I found myself back in Cairo, Egypt. Three of my girl friends wanted to go, and I thought after all these years I would like to return. I really loved Egypt when Don and I lived there, and felt I was finally ready to see it again. We had just finished having lunch and I approached the maitre'd in the lobby. "The meal was wonderful, and the hotel is exquisite," I said. "Excuse me madam, but I don't work here. My name is Gharbi Abdelmajid, I'm a diplomat from Tunisia," he stated. I felt so silly, but we talked a while and he was very nice. We stayed in touch and began writing each other often. I don't know what I was thinking, but perhaps I needed a little romantic fantasy, a foreign intrigue.

It moved beyond fantasy when he invited me to come visit, and a few months later I arrived in Tunisia. I was his guest at the grandest hotel in Tunis, and unlike the cowboy in McAllen Texas, he had no picnic food in a suitcase. In fact, he had no suitcase at all as he had no intention of trying to stay in my room. This was a very traditional place; women didn't walk the streets unescorted there, it wasn't considered proper. But the hotel was like a palace, so I didn't mind spending most of my time indoors.

Gharbi was a gentleman: very polite and refined. He threw lavish parties while I was there, inviting friends and family. They were all very nice to me. And why not, I was the guest of honor, though I didn't know it. Everyone was there to meet the woman Gharbi was to marry—me! The only problem in his wedding plans is that he didn't bother to ask me if I wanted to married him until long after the parties were over. Under different circumstances, I might have actually considered it. But, we were from different worlds, different cultures, and I told him it could never work. Still, he insisted—to the point that I became a little nervous. I was on foreign soil, in a country where women had very few rights, and he was a diplomat after all. So I told him that I would strongly consider marrying him, but first needed to return to New York. We stayed in touch and continued to write, but of course I never went back, and eventually, I stopped writing.

Looking back I had many famous or influential suitors, Gaharbi the Tunisian diplomat, John Jacob Astor III the aristocrat, and John Roosevelt the son of a president. I also had a bit of a romp with a young handsome man who was temporarily in New York studying law during my Copa days. My friend Virginia set it up because she was dating the man's friend (who I later learned was his body guard). It was all a little mysterious to me that no one would discuss where he was from, his background or anything. The next seventy-two hours was definitely a "live for today" crazy weekend where we wined, dinned and danced. Twenty years later (during the 1960s) I was reading the New York Times, only to discover that my date was a Prince, who had just become a King. Now that's what I call "a royal screwing!" Still, Don was the love of my life, and i shared fourteen wonderful years with George. You get many opportunities in life, but the ones you act on are the only one's that matter: after all, what's done is done. I wouldn't have traded my time with Don or George for anything— not even royalty.

I have continued to stay active attending parties and events. Why not? I'm still breathing, thanks to a pacemaker I had installed last December. I get together with Nikki, Rosie, and Roxanne regularly. They remain my connection to Clovis, and he continues to live in their presence as they retell old stories like they were brand new. Roxanne had been a successful photographer, working for Armani, Vogue, Glamour and others for years. But it was the famous people she photographed, up close and personal, candidly, that would be the images for her book entitled, "People." In 2002 the publisher gave her a book party at Lot 61, a very trendy spot on the Westside. I loved it!

That same year, John Juliano reopened the Copacabana in yet another new location on west 34th Street, diagonally across the street from the Jacob Javitz Convention Center. Most people would have given up on the Copa, but not John. He had been successful in all his other endeavors, and was committed to reviving the Copa name. He was savvy enough to reinvent the club for the masses this time, using the Copa name and theme, but in a huge facility 50,000 square feet, on three levels: a contrast to the original club's intimate lounge and showroom geared for the high society crowd. John finally obtained the success for the Copa name that had eluded him for so many years.

The press was hosting interviews with famous people outside the club, and the invite only crowd got a sense of the glitz and glamour of by-gone era. The new club, though inspired by the original—with its Latin themes, and famous Copa logo painted on the wall—had significant differences. For one thing, the "big" room really was big! Probably four times the size of the original. The stage alone was large enough to fit a 10-piece band without difficulty. Today crowds pack the dance floor weekly dancing to Latin music.

Before their debut, the new Copa girls huddled around me asking questions faster than I could respond. Most of them looked like babies, barely out of their teens, if that. "What was the original Copa like? Did you meet famous people? Who were your favorites? What were the costumes like? It was over-whelming; the questions were coming from all angles. I loved it! The press interviewed me too—that's what happens when you're the last living member of the original anything, everyone wants one final glimpse of the past. Even the Governor made an appearance. I was having the time of my life, again. Even though the Copa is a different kind of club these days, it still evokes memories for me: a once upon a time story when I was in the chorus line at the COPACABANA.

CHAPTER 20

Espionage and Other Mysteries

Fifty plus years after the crash that killed my husband (Don), I was contacted by Charlotte Dennett. She had read a story in the Army Times about my missing furniture, which noted my husband's plane crash, and when she saw the date of the crash realized that my husband and her father were probably on the same plane. She phoned me immediately, and within two weeks we were comparing notes in my living room. She told me her father (Daniel Dennett) was a United States cultural attaché in Lebanon during the war. But that was just his cover. He was actually a spy, an expert in counter-intelligence for the Office of Strategic Services and Central Intelligence Group, which were the immediate predecessors to the CIA.

Charlotte too had many unanswered questions about her father's death, and like me, felt that there was more to the story. Sensitive information that had been held secret for all these years had recently been de-classified, and Charlotte and her husband, Jerry Colby, obtained a copy of the official accident report from the National Archives in College Point, Maryland. However, the report—having many inconsistencies—produced more questions than answers.

The accident report said there were four flight-crew members (including Don), plus Daniel Dennett (cultural attaché), Lt. Creech (Office of the US Secretary of War), and Donald Sullivan (petroleum attaché) aboard the plane when it crashed in the mountains of Ethiopia. Col. McNown, a US military attaché, was aboard for earlier legs of the trip, but not when it crashed, and that too had suspicious undertones.

I told Charlotte and Jerry what happened to me on the day before the crash. The morning of March 19th, without any advance warning of the flight, Don and I were woken up early to find members of his unit and flight crew in our house ready to be served breakfast. He wasn't scheduled to go, but at the last minute was assigned to the mission as the flight radio engineer. He turned to one of his friends, pointed to me (I was eight months pregnant) and said, "Take care of her." He hugged me and whispered that he loved me. It was the last time I ever saw him.

Charlotte told me she and Jerry were writing a book that included the circumstances leading up to the crash. She explained that they had to do a lot of background research on Saudi Arabia and Ethiopia in 1945–1947 to fully understand the possible cause of what happened and why. That required understanding the main players and their objectives being played out after World War II in Africa and the Middle East. There were three major powers, she explained, Britain, Russia and the United States, all competing for influence in the Middle East and Africa, and specifically Libya, Saudi Arabia and Ethiopia. In summary, the objective of the big three was a geopolitical chess game for strategic military positioning, and of course, oil—which by this time was referred to as "wartime ammunition."

With this in mind, we went over some of the facts that emerged from the accident report: When the plane arrived in Jidda, Saudi Arabia on the 19th, Asmara (the next stop in Eritrea) called ahead to inquire as to whether the plane would continue on to that location. Jidda replied, "no." But, the plane did in fact arrive in Asmara "without warning." To date it is still not known who in Jidda provided the false information, or why the plane flew under a blanket of secrecy to Asmara. When the plane then left Asmara en route back to Addis (the leg of the trip when the plane crashed), a message proceeded the flight saying, "USATC C47 DEPARTED FOR ADDIS 06:15. ETA: 0900. **US MILITARY ATTACHE ON BOARD.**" But, in fact, Colonel McNown (the US Military Attaché) wasn't onboard. At the last possible moment, he remained behind. We couldn't help but wonder why?

In Colonel McNown's section of the accident report, he noted that from the time the plane did not arrive in Addis (and for the next 24 hours that followed), there was no overdue action consistent with a missing plane. Also puzzling is that Felix Cole, the US Minister in Addis, did not send out an overdue notice until 24 hours after the crash, even though he must have known the plane was missing when American embassy cars returned from the Addis airport on March 20th having failed to meet the plane, which had been scheduled to arrive around noon on the 20th. And for some strange reason, his telegram to Washington on the morning of the 21st alerting the State Department that there were no survivors, did not reach Cairo, Jidda and Teheran (which were much closer to Ethiopia) until late in the afternoon of March 21st.

Colonel McNown noted at the beginning of his report that "all observations and factual evidence point to pilot error though it is extremely difficult to believe that a pilot of Lt. Smith's ability and experience could have had an accident of this type." Lt. Col. C.L. Nothstein, who had flown hundred's of hours with Smith, described Smith as "the most sensible, displayed more judgment and was the pilot least apt to get into trouble, while flying, of all those assigned this unit. I had implicit faith in his knowledge and techniques and feel certain that the recent accident in which he and his crew were killed occurred from some other cause than his ability and judgment as a pilot."

The official Military story:

1) <u>The plane was carrying heavy freight and ran into bad weather</u>: However, the accident report shows the weather report as clear upon takeoff, that no one in the plane had on seat belts, the landing gear was not down, the flaps were not down, the propellers were not feathered—indicating that there was no apparent concern by the pilots of being in trouble.

2) <u>There was a pilot error</u>: However, the same accident report admits that the pilot had no schedule to maintain, no real necessity to complete the mission at any certain time, and there were several routes the pilot could have taken. Thus, there seems to have been no reason for this flight to be unsafe or encounter any circumstances by which the plane should have faced any difficulty—unless there was a sudden and dramatic weather change. All those that knew the pilot considered the accident improbable, however a sudden change in weather—particularly heavy cloud cover—though improbable, is plausible.

3) <u>The maps were off</u>: However, Lt. Smith had flown the route before and therefore would have been very well aware of any maps that were not accurate.

Questions that arise after reading the declassified report:

1) Documents being carried by Lt. Creech were labeled, "top secret," suggesting that this was not, as reported, a "routine mission."

2) Except for Asmara, none of the U.S. or British controlled bases in Saudi Arabia, Ethiopia and Sudan registered any concern over a missing plane until late in the afternoon on the 21st, leaving any rational person to ask, why?

3) Minister Cole, the Ambassador at Addis, did not report a missing plane that had several US diplomats aboard to Washington until 24 hours after he must have known the plane was missing. Why did he delay?

4) Why did the plane fly under cover from Jidda to Asmara?

5) Why did Asmara report Colonel McNown to be aboard, when he wasn't?

6) For that matter, why did Colonel McNown stay off the plane at the last minute?

Britain, Russia, and the United States were engaged in clandestine maneuvers to control land, oil and relationships in Eastern Africa and the Middle East. It would appear that this flight mission was involved, or somehow got tangled up, in a much larger plot being played out. The British, who controlled Ethiopia during World War II, were jealous of American inroads being made in Ethiopia after the war, especially in the field of air travel, telecommunications and oil exploration. But Dennett and Colby have also discovered that the Russians were playing a bigger role in Ethiopia than they had previously realized, and that there is some evidence that they were trying to make inroads in signal/radio communications, including those used by airplanes, at the time of the crash.

Of course, it is possible that the plane ran into a freak storm. Such things have been known to happen in the mountains of Ethiopia. But I have a hard time believing that it was a mere accident, especially with the gaps in the accident report and the fact that all the passengers had high-level intelligence clearance, and other things that I am not at liberty to print here. Through documents obtained by Dennett and Colby, I now know that that my husband, along with engineer Holm and Colonel McNown were all with military intelligence. It appears that Lt. Creech was as well.

Perhaps Dennett and Colby's forthcoming book, *The Kingdom and The Power: Oil, the Holocaust, and American Espionage at the Dawn of the Middle East Crisis,* due to be published in 2006 will shed more light on how and why the plane crashed. Until then I may never get concrete answers as to why my husband died. To this day my personal effects and the officer in charge of them remain missing. This may just one of those unsolved mysteries that you think, "that could never happen to me!"

CHAPTER 21

Life Is Like That

It was early morning and I had just finished breakfast. I climbed back into bed to read the paper—the television on low in the background. It's part of my routine. I don't sleep more than three to four hours a night, and I'm up at the crack of dawn. When I heard the words, "Wrap dress," my ears perked up. I focused on the television and saw Diane Von Furstenberg being interviewed about a new (at that time) soon-to-be-released book entitled *The Wrap*. When she claimed that she invented the design, I was furious. With a little diligence I reached her secretary and told her I wanted to talk to Diane.

When she called back I told her, "Diane, you didn't invent the wrap dress, Clovis did!" Her response was causal, "Nothing in fashion is really new Harriet; everything has always been done before. I was inspired to create the wrap dress from the Japanese kimono." That seemed a little convenient to me. After all, there are dozens of people who knew that Clovis was creating patterns for his wrap dress design in 1969, years before Diane even had her label. Not to mention that by 1972 he won the Coty award for fashion at a price, in part, because of that dress. "Listen Diane, let my son rest in peace and retain the accomplishments of his career! He may be dead, but I'm not, and I'm here to protect his interests!" And that was all I had to say about that!

People tell me, "Harriet, slow down, take it easy," and I tell them I'll be dead a long time—I can take it easy then. I never understood what it is people are resting up for. I have girlfriends that won't go out because it's raining, it's snowing, it's too cold, or it's too hot. Get over it, life is short and when a day is gone, it's gone forever, you can't get it back. I continue to live every day, that's my motto. Just yesterday I went to dinner with my friend Richard. We've been friends since the 1960s: we met at an art class George and I enrolled in. When Clovis was sick and fell in the middle of the night, it was Richard I called, and he came to my aid without hesitation. He's always been a true friend, and I love him for that. We have dinner every Saturday night, but on this occasion, I had the air conditioner man at my apartment taking off the covers the night before. As luck would have it, it fell, and smashed my toe. My bones are very fragile. I can break a rib just from a friend giving me too strong of a hug, or opening or closing a window at the wrong angle. I was scheduled to meet Richard in an hour, but I couldn't put a shoe or a sock on my foot. So I got a plastic bag, put it over my foot and secured it with a rubber band, and away we went. Should I have stayed in because my toe was swollen? Don't be ridiculous!

Maybe it's my lack of fear that has been the catalyst for so many experiences. Some were more pleasurable than others, but I just don't know any other way to live. I leave for Buenos Aires, Argentina two days from now. I don't walk very well these days, but one way or another I'll make it. This will make my nineteenth trip in seventeen years. My friend Brie will be there to meet me, and we'll have a toast to the completion of this book. I met Brie late one night at a local coffee shop in my neighborhood. We lived just a few blocks from each other. From the first night we met in 2001 we have been good friends. Who could have known he would turn out to be a writer and help me complete my book? At the same time, I urged him to accompany me to Buenos Aires in 2003, and he loved it so much that he now lives there. It just goes to show the impact that accidental friendships and spur of the moment choices can have on the direction of one's life.

I still live for the nightlife, and there isn't a party or affair that I'm invited to that I don't attend. The nightlife is what I love about Buenos Aires. People flock to the outdoor café's in the many plazas. Having dinner at 10:00, 11:00 or 12:00-midnight is common. There are clubs open until the sun comes up; that's my kind of town, and Buenos Aires is one of the few left.

My life is closing in on a century of living. I hope it has been entertaining, and perhaps you gained some insights to things you didn't know about, especially the 40s and 50s. That was my favorite era. I miss it and some days I sit at my kitchen table, close my eyes and just listen to my cassettes. Recently, I had a pleasant surprise. I received a call and I was invited to experience a 1940s styled supper club in New Jersey. "New Jersey?" I said. The owner wanted my impression of its authenticity, promised that it would be worth the ride and sent a car for me. I must say it was fabulous. I was quite impressed. If what you have read in this book intrigues you about that era, stop in at Richie Cecere's Restaurant & Supper Club in Montclair, New Jersey, just west of Manhattan (call ahead for a reservation!). It is like going back in time.

I have lived though several distinctly different eras of American life. I have seen many things, met great people and had my share of adventures. I experienced true love, loss, sorrow, joy, and exhilaration. But it's life, all of it, the good and the bad. And given the chance, you know what? Of course you do…*I'd do it again!*

978-0-595-36492-3
0-595-36492-6

Printed in the United States
36914LVS00004B/40

9 780595 364923